MACHINE LEARNING

WITH PYTHON

Step By Step Methods To Master
Machine Learning With Python

ALEXANDER CANE

Table of Contents

Introduction

Thank you for choosing my guide, "Machine Learning with Python: Step By Step Methods To Master Machine Learning With Python."

Machine learning is one of the current buzzwords, and it's safe to say it is the future. My guide will walk you through the core machine learning concepts using Python. You should already have some knowledge of the Python programming language but I have started the guide with a quick Python primer.

In chapter two, we look at the machine learning basics. This will give you the background you need and a solid base from which to start your machine learning journey. I will teach you the types of machine learning models, particularly the Artificial Neural Network, or ANN. We also talk terminology; it is very important that you understand the terms you will read and hear about.

In chapter three, we move on to machine learning algorithms, and we look at some of the more popular once I've kept things simple here and you won't need any background in coding to understand this chapter. We'll be talking about supervised learning algorithms, unsupervised learning algorithms and reinforcement learning, the three types of algorithm that serve as the backbone for all the other learning algorithms that are being developed right now.

Chapter four deals with pre-processing the data and creating training data sets. This is the part of machine learning that takes the most time and is the most imperative to get right. I will walk you through the stages needed to complete preprocessing and splitting data into training and testing data sets, to make sure you have a thorough understanding.

In chapter five, we move onto Scikit-Learn, one of the most popular machine learning libraries. I will walk you through using Scikit-Learn, using real code that you can try – at the end of the day, the only real way to learn is to get on and do it. We'll also look at solving common, nonlinear problems with kernel trick algorithms and k-nearest neighbor.

In chapter six, we'll get to grips with TensorFlow and use it to build neural networks. You will learn everything you need to know, using open-source data and real code. TensorFlow has been built on Python, which is why it is so perfect for the job. It is a simple architecture, flexible, and easily provides for taking a machine learning idea from just that, an idea right through to code, on to building fantastic models and publication, all in a short time.

And, for our final chapter, we look at six tips that you must follow to build a solid data training strategy. Without a strategy, your systems will not work; this is one of the most important steps in any project – forget the strategy, you might as well forget building your machine learning model.

We end the guide with a quiz. But, I don't want you to panic here. There are 25 multiple choice questions, but don't worry if you don't know the answer. While some answers will be here, in this guide, the quiz will help you identify areas that you need to practice more, and areas that you can look at in your next stage of machine learning mastery.

Why Use Python?

It's clear that the future is all about artificial intelligence and machine learning. We all want better recommendations, better personalization, and we want much more from our internet searches. The apps we use can see, they can hear, and they can even respond, and that is a direct result of artificial intelligence – improving the user experience and bringing much more value across every industry.

This brings two questions to mind, though – How do we bring those experiences to life and what's the best computer programming language to use?

The obvious answer is to use Python because it is the best language for machine learning.

Why?

What makes it the best programming language?

Artificial intelligence projects are different from your standard software project, and that difference comes from the technology stack, from the skills that you need for artificial intelligence projects and from the real necessity for deep research.

You need a programming language that offers stability, flexibility, and a wide range of tools. Python gives you all this and more. From development, right through deployment to maintenance, the Python language helps us to be productive developers, confident about what we are building.

The main benefits of using Python for machine learning are:

Simplicity and Consistency

Python gives us code that is readable and concise. While complex algorithms and workflows back machine learning and artificial intelligence, the fact that Python is so simple is what lets us develop reliable systems. As developers, you can put everything you have into solving your machine learning problems rather than having to focus on learning the technicalities of the programming language.

Not only that, Python is one of the easiest programming languages to learn – it is human-readable, and that makes it far easier to produce machine learning models.

Lots of programmers are in agreement that Python offers more intuitive programming than any other language while others will tell you that the libraries, frameworks, and extensions are the high point as they simplify the process of implementing lots of different functionalities,

Typically, most developers accept that Python is perfect for collaborative implementation when several developers work on one project, and because it is an all-purpose language, it can do plenty of highly complex tasks in machine learning and let you quickly build your prototypes for testing your machine learning products.

Vast Choice of Frameworks and Libraries

Machine learning and artificial intelligence algorithms are not the easiest to implement, and they take no small amount of time. The environment has to be structured properly and tested to ensure that developers can produce the best solutions.

To help reduce the time needed, Python offers loads of frameworks and libraries. The libraries are code that has already been written, providing developers with an easy solution to common tasks in programming. With one of the richest technology stacks, Python offers a large number of libraries for both machine learning and artificial intelligence. Some of the best are:

- Scikit-learn, TensorFlow, and Keras for machine learning

- NumPy for data analysis and scientific performance

- SciPy for more advanced computing

- Seaborn for data visualization

- Pandas for data analysis

In Scikit-learn, there are several algorithms – regression, classification, and clustering – including the random forests, support vector machines, k-means, gradient boosting, and DBSCAN. It is also perfectly designed for working with the scientific and numerical libraries, SciPy and NumPy.

Using these, your machine learning product can be developed much faster; there's no need for reinventing the wheel, and the libraries are there for all the required features.

What Python is Good For

Below you can see all the common artificial intelligence use cases and the best technology for them:

Use Case	Library/Framework
Visualization and data analysis	SciPy, Seaborn, NumPy, Pandas
Machine learning	Scikit-learn, Keras, TensorFlow
Computer vision	OpenCV
Natural Language Processing (NLP)	spaCy, NLTK

Python is Platform Independent

That means whatever you implement on one machine can easily be used on another with little to no changes. One of the most crucial points to the popularity of Python is that it is supported on multiple platforms, including Windows, Linux, and macOS. You can use code to build standalone code for all the popular operating systems, and that makes Python a distributable software that can be used on any of the platforms without the need for a Python interpreter.

Many developers use Amazon or Google for their computing requirements, but some data scientists and companies have their own machines designed with the most powerful GPUs for training machine learning models. And, because Python is a platform-independent language, the training is easier and cheaper.

Incredibly Popular and an Active Community

In 2018, Stack Overflow published a Developer Survey showing Python as being in the top ten popular languages, and it is the computer language googled more often than any other.

One of the biggest use cases of Python is for web development, but machine learning and data science are fast catching up. Online repositories account for around 140,000 software packages, custom-built in Python and scientific packages, such as SciPy, NumPy, and Matplotlib can easily be installed on any program that runs on Python. These are the important packages for Machine learning, packages that allow us to examine large sets of data and find the patterns. Such is Python's reliability that Google uses it to crawl through web pages, Spotify uses it for their track recommendation engine and Pixar uses it in the movies they produce.

And it is well-known that the Python artificial intelligence community is huge, spreading right around the globe. A quick internet search will bring up tons of Python forums, where you can get help, chat about code, or share your own knowledge and experience. No matter what you are trying to do with Python, it's a fair bet that someone else has answers you might need.

That's the thing about Python; you are never alone as a developer, and you can always find the answers within the community.

If you're ready to start your journey, let's dive right in.

Chapter 1

Python Primer

Back in 1989, Guido van Rossum, a Dutch programmer working for Google at the time, developed the Python programming language. For a long time, it didn't really take off as a language but, since artificial intelligence and machine learning have become such big parts of our lives, so Python grew in popularity.

If you are aiming to be a data scientist and you choose just one programming language to learn, make it Python. It is the language for data exploration, extracting data, analyzing it and visualizing it.

And it's really quite an easy language to learn. I'm going to assume that, as you are reading a guide about machine learning with Python, you already have some familiarity with the language, but, as a quick primer, I'm going to run over the basics of Python programming language before we dive into machine learning.

This is a very basic look, and, for those of you who do have the experience, you might want to skip this. What we are going to do as look at functions, variables, conditions, loops, and all the other basics you need knowledge of to get into machine learning, plus a few data structures for the efficient storage and processing of data.

First off, Python is what we call an interpreted language. That means, as soon as your code is written, the Python compiler begins executing it, one line at a time, starting at the top.

If you want to play along, you need one of two things – Python installed on your computer or a Python notebook, such as Jupyter or Google Colab, both free. The best way to learn is to get practical so do play about with the code so you understand it and what it can do.

There are two versions of Python – v2 and v3. Stick with using v3; it is the latest, and it has more support than the earlier version.

That's enough of all that, let's dive into Python.

Your First Program

```
# Showing "Hello World!" on your screen
# print is a default function, already defined in
Python; we're just using it
print("Hello World!")
```

The first two lines are comments. A Python comment is a note, if you like, explaining what a piece of code or program is doing. They must start with a hash (#) sign and will not be executed. It's a good idea to get into the habit of writing short, meaningful comments, not just for your benefit but for others who read your code.

The third line is the program, telling the computer to print "Hello World!" on your screen. And, when you run that program, that is exactly what you will see on your screen.

The print function is a built-in function already defined by Python, and you will use it many times, along with other built-in functions, all helping to make life easier for you.

Programming Styles

Before we go any further, you need to be aware that there three ways of writing code in Python:

- Unstructured

- Procedural

- Object-oriented

With unstructured programming, the code is written as one monolithic file. When you are writing large programs, though, you should be using the unstructured programming style. It's fine for small pieces of code like you will see in this chapter because is it convenient.

With procedural programming, code is grouped into functions, and there are two steps to the process:

1. Define or write the function

2. Invoke or call the function

The function is written once, and then you can call it as many times as needed. This is another style of programming you will see in this chapter.

With object-oriented programming, blueprints are identified, and a class is created for each one.

Don't worry if you don't understand so far; you will as we go on.

Variables

Variables are described as containers or placeholders where data is stored in memory.

There are basic data types in Python, and using those you can create numerical variables, i.e., floats or integers, and string variables. Depending on which type you create, Python allocates a certain amount of memory.

Unlike other programming languages, Python does not require you to specify what the data type is when you create a variable. Instead, Python infers it automatically, based on the value. For that reason, Python is known as a 'dynamically typed' language.

I will assume that you are using Python 3 on your computer. Let's do some interactive coding. Open a shell (Windows Command Prompt) or a terminal if using Mac or Unix-based systems. At the prompt, type python and you will see something like this:

```
$ python3.6
Python 3.6.1 (v3.6.1:69c0db5050, Dec 01 2019, 01:21:04)
[GCC 4.2.1 (Apple Inc. build 5666) (dot 3)] on darwin
```

Type "help", "copyright", "credits" or "license" for more information.

```
>>>
```

Now we can explore some variables:

```
#integer variable
>>> x = 50
>>> print(x)
50
```

The variable named x stores a value, 50. 50 is an integer, so Python automatically infers it as type int (integer).

Here's another one:

The variable, name, is storing a value of 'Annie' and, because this is a string, it is inferred as a type string.

Another one:

```
#assigning several times
>>> x = 50
>>> x = 15
>>> print(x)
15
```

When variable values are assigned several times, the older value will be replaced with the newer one. In the example above, the value of 50 is replaced by 15. There can only ever be a single placeholder for x at any time.

Strings and Numbers

As well as the integer data type, Python also provides support for other numerical types, like the floating-point numbers. Here's an example:

```
#floating point numbers
>>> z = 1.58
>>> print(z)
1.58
```

Any numerical variable will support any of the standard mat operations, like subtraction, addition, division, multiplication, and modulus:

```
# Numerical operations
>>> a = 20
>>> b = 40
```

```
#addition
>>> print(a+b)
60
 #subtraction
>>> print(a-b)
-20
#division
>>> print(a/b)
0.5
#modulus
>>> print(b%a)
0
```

Let's look at strings.

#define the string variable called firstname and assign a value "Antony."

```
>>> firstname = "Antony"
#print string
>>> print(firstname)
Antony
#print first character of string variable
>>> print(firstname[0])
A
#print second character of string variable
>>> print(firstname[1])
n
#print length of string
>>> print(len(firstname))
6
#print first, second characters
>>> print(firstname[0:2])
An
```

```
#print second and third characters
>>> print(firstname[1:3])
nt
```

Strings act much like character arrays, data structures holding several values of matching type. In the above example, the array is firstname, holding six characters – A, n, t, o, n, y. the index begins at 0 so, when you want the first element, you would ask for

```
firstname[0]
```

Here's a few more examples:

```
#string concatenation (combining two or more strings)
>>> lastname = "Hopkins"
>>> fullname = firstname + " " + lastname
>>> print(fullname)
Antony Hopkins
```

Here, our variable called fullname combines or concatenates three strings – firstname, lastname and a constant string of ", "

Functions

Functions are blocks of code, organized to be repeatedly used just by invoking the function name. The print() function we used earlier, for example, takes an argument, and it prints that argument onto your screen. And the len() function also takes an argument of an array or a list and prints the number of elements in the array/list. Keep in mind that strings are arrays and len() gives the number of characters the string contains.

A function syntax is:

```
def function_name(arguments):
    <function body>
```

Here, def is a keyword that indicates you want to define a function, function_name is the name of the function you are defining. Typically, it will be a name that describes what the function does, such as print(). If, for example, you had a function used for calculating business tax, you might call it something like calculate_tax.

The arguments are the input parameters. Functions can have zero or more; for example, the print() function and the len() function both take one argument.

Lastly, function_body is where the Python statements go, and they must have the function name attached so Python knows which function the code belongs to.

Functions don't have to return values. The len() function does; it returns that input parameter length. The print() function, on the other hand, doesn't return a value; all it does is prints the argument to screen.

```
#define function
def add(x, y):
  result = x + y
  return the result

#use the function
return_value = add(20, 30)
```

```
print(return_value)

#and another example
print(add(6, 12))
```

The short code example above is defining add, a very simple function that takes two arguments of x and y. Inside the function_body, we add two input arguments we want to be added. Because we are using a mathematical operation, the function will expect the parameters to be numerical. Then we ask for the value to be returned. Note, the word 'return' is a reserved keyword in Python and is only used for returning a function's value, nothing else.

Next, we passed some different arguments, reusing the same function and get a different value printed.

As I said earlier, don't expect every function to return values. If you were to call the following function:

```
def foo():
    print("This function won't return a value")
```
the output would be

```
>>>foo()
```

This function won't return a value

Functions that don't return values typically just print to the screen, which is not returning values. If you want a function to return a value, you must include a return() statement.

Conditions

Conditions are used for making decisions between two paths.

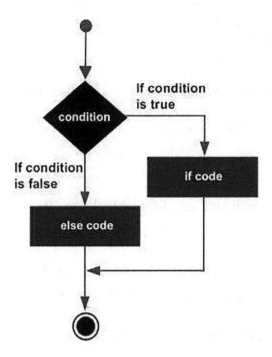

The diagram above demonstrates an if-else control block, and, as you can see, Python will execute the if-code ONLY if the condition evaluates true. If it doesn't, the else-code is executed.

```
def test_condition(x):
    if x == 1:
        print("GREAT!")
    else:
        print("NOT SO GREAT!")
```

Note that the code above also makes use of functions.

What we have here is

So we have:

function

```
       |
       |_____   if-else block in the function
```

What do you think would happen if you called test_condition(1)?

```
>>>test_condition(1)
```

GREAT!

The function contains an if-else block, so, if x=1, GREAT! is printed. If it doesn't. NOT SO GREAT! is printed instead.

This condition is known as a Boolean expression. Booleans only have two possible outcomes – TRUE or FALSE.

If the condition evaluates TRUE, the if-code is executes

If it evaluates FALSE, the else-code is evaluated.

So, what would we get if we called test_condition(5)?

You should have got that one:

```
>>>test_condition(5)
```

NOT SO GREAT!

Here are a few other examples of conditions containing Boolean expressions:

```
x == y → checks the value to see if the x value is
equal to the y value
x > y → check to see if x is more than y
name == "Antony" → checks to see if the name is equal
to Antony
len(name) == 6 → checks to see if the string variable
length is  6
```

Loops

Typically, Python code is executed, top to bottom, in sequence. You can, however, run one block of code over and again, by using a loop. Python has two primary loops – the while loop and the for loop. Let's look at both of them.

while Loop

The syntax for a while loop is

```
while (condition):
    code-block
```

When the condition evaluates true, the code will be executed over and over, until the condition evaluates false.

Here's an example:

```
x = 0
while x < 4:
    x = x + 2
    print(x)
```

What would the output be?

The condition, x < 4, will evaluate true for as long as x remains less than 4. While it does, the code within the while loop is executed.

At the start, x is equal to 0, so the condition is true. Then, we have the line, x = x + 2 so, on the first loop 2 is added to 0, making it 2, and x is printed, which is 2.

Control then goes back to the start of the while loop, and the condition is evaluated once more. Now, x is 2 and, because it is still less than 4, the condition is still true. Again, it is incremented by 2 making x become 4, which is what gets printed.

On the next go around, x will become 4, and the condition will evaluate false because x will no longer be less than 4. At that point, the while loop stops being executed.

Have a look at the next code; what do you think the output will be?

```
x = 12
while x > 0:
    print(x)
    x = x - 3
```

for loop

Another loop often used is the for loop, and the syntax is:

```
for <a collection value> in <some collection>:
    code-block
```

Let's see an example to understand that. Before we do, though, we need to look at another function built into Python – the range() function. This function is used for creating sequences of numbers. Here are a couple of examples:

```
range(1, 6)
```

A sequence is created, containing 1, 2, 3, 4, 5 – note that the last number, 6, is not included.

Here's another example:

```
range(0, 12, 3)
```

The third argument, 3, is the size of the step – if you don't specify it, the default is 1. This example would print 0, 3, 6, 9

This can be used to write our while loop from earlier with a for loop.

```
for x in range(1, 4):
    print(x)
```

And the second example:

```
for x in range(12, 0, -3):
    print(x)
```

Later, we'll see some other cool ways the for loop is used.

Libraries

Libraries are useful for giving us the functionality we can use straight away. The sheer number of libraries available in Python is one of the reasons why it is has grown in popularity. Think of something you might want to do, and there's a god chance Python has a library for it.

Let's say, for example, that you wanted command-line arguments read. A standard Python library, called sys, helps you do that. Before you can use it, you must import it into your program, and then you can use the functions included in it.

First, we'll assume you have a new file, named first.py, and you want the first command-line argument printed:

```
import sysfirst_argument = sys.argv[1]
print(first_argument)
```

Now, you simply run the following program:

```
python first.py Hello
```

The first argument's value, in this case, 'Hello,' is stored in sys.argv[1]. The output on the screen would be Hello.

As you get to grips with Python, you will get to know many libraries, such as Matplotlib, Pandas, Scikit-learn, NumPy, and many more.

Let's now create a program with two command-line arguments – we'll call this one second.py:

sys.argv[1] stores the value of the first argument, which is "Hello." So, your program will print Hello on the screen.

```
import sys
first_argument = sys.argv[1]
second_argument = sys.argv[2]
print("{} {}".format(first_argument,
second_argument))
```

And the code is run like this:

```
python second.py Hello World!
```

And the output?

It should be Hello World! because argument 1 is Hello, and argument 2 is World!

Data Structures - Lists

Lists are used to hold values, and they can all be of different types. For example, you could create a list containing both string and integer values. A list is mutable, which means, once created, you can add to it or remove from it.

Here is an example:

```
# A list containing values
names = ["Annie", "Barry", "Evelyn", "Antony",
"Marjorie"]
```

An empty list can be created like this:

```
names = list()
```

You can use append() to add new items at the end of the list:

```
names.append("Thomas")
names.append("Mary")
print(names)
```

And the output would be

```
["Thomas", "Mary"]
```

You can also iterate through lists:

```
names = ["Thomas", "Mary", "Antony"]
```

for name in names:

```
print("Student: {}".format(name))
```

With the output being:

```
Student: Thomas
Student: Mary
Student: Antony
```

Note how the for loop is written. Each item is picked by the loop and assigned to a variable named as 'name.' That variable can then be used to write business logic in your loop.

Here's another example:

```
# A list containing numbers
```

```
ages = [22, 31, 26, 29, 33, 39, 30, 21, 28]
```

How would we work out the average age?

We would need to sum, or add, the values and then divide the result by the number of entries in the list. We use the len() function to see how many entries there are:

```
count = len(ages)
sum = 0
for age in ages:
    sum = sum + age
avg = sum / count
print("Average age is {}".format(avg))
```

And the output would be:

```
Average age is 28.7777777778
```

Here's the full code example:

```
ages = [22, 31, 26, 29, 33, 39, 30, 21, 28]
count = len(ages)
sum = 0
```

for age in ages:

```
    sum = sum + age
avg = sum / count
print("Average age is {}".format(avg))
```

Let's break down what happened here, using line numbers to describe each line of code:

Line 1 – a list is defined, named 'ages' and age values used to initialize it

Line 2 – use the len() function to count how many entries are in the list and store the result in a variable named 'count.'

Line 3 – a variable named 'sum' is initialized to zero, and we will use this for summing up the age values

Line 4 – in the line header code, each entry is taken from the list and assigned to 'age.'

Line 5 – the current value of 'age' is added to 'sum' in every loop iteration

Line 6 – now we have come out of the for loop, and we just take the average of all the ages

Line 7 – the average is printed to screen

Data Structures - Sets

Python sets are much like lists with the exception that only unique values may be stored in a set – a list may contain duplicate entries.

```
# set containing initial values
coin_sides = {"Head", "Tail"}# an empty set
colors = set()
```

Here is a list and a set beside each other:

```
>>> myset = set()
>>> mylist = list()>>> myset.add("Pineapple")
>>> mylist.append("Pineapple")>>> print(myset)
{'Pineapple'}>>> print(mylist)
['Pineapple']
```

What happens if Pineapple is added to both again?

```
>>> myset.add("Pineapple")
>>> mylist.append("Pineapple")
>>> print(myset)
{'Pineapple'}
>>> print(mylist)
['Pineapple', 'Pineapple']
```

A set will keep just one copy of every different value while a list will retain all of them, even the duplicates.

```
>>> myset.add("Guava")
>>> mylist.append("Guava")
>>> print(myset)
{'Guava', 'Pineapple'}
>>> print(mylist)
['Pineapple', 'Pineapple', 'Guava']
```

And looping would be the same as it is with looping a list

for fruit in myset:

```
print(fruit)
```

And the output would be:

```
Guava
Pineapple
```

Data Structures - Dictionary

The Python dictionary is a type of data structure that lets us store key-value pairs. For example:

```
students = {"Annie":10, "Antony": 5}
```

The dictionary is called 'students,' and it has two entries. The keys are "Annie" and "Antony" and the values, 10 and 5.

Here's another way a dictionary is created:

```
students = dict()
students["Annie"] = 10
students["Antony"] = 5
```

Iterating a Dictionary:

```
for key, value in students.items():
    print("Key = {} Value = {}".format(key, value))
```

The output will be:

```
Key = Annie Value = 10
Key = Antony Value = 5
```

And another way of iterating a dictionary, although this isn't so efficient so it isn't really encouraged:

for key in students:

```
print("Key = {} Value = {}".format(key, students[key]))
```

The output is exactly the same as above.

File I/O

To finish our primer, we'll look at File I/O, something you need to know for data science and machine learning. Let's look at the basic operations:

Assume we have a file named data.csv, and in it are these values, separated with commas:

```
Annie,10
Antony,5
Mary,8
file_handle = open("data.csv", "r")
```

for line in file_handle:
```
values = line.split(",")
print("Name = {} Age = {}".format(values[0], values[1]))
file_handle.close()
```

Line 1 – the file called data.csv is opened for reading (r)

Line 3 – each of the lines in the file is iterated through with each line being copied to a variable named "line."

Line 4 – the value of the 'line' variable is split by "," creating an array containing two elements. The array is stored inside the "values" variable

Line 5 – the two values are printed

Line 7 – the file is closed

The output would look like this:

```
Name = Annie Age = 10
Name = Antony Age = 5
Name = Mary Age = 8
```

And we can write the same code in a different way, this time using 'with,' another keyword. Here, we won't call the close() method:

```
with open("data.csv", "r") as file_handle:
    for line in file_handle:
        values = line.split(",")
        print("Name = {} Age = {}".format(values[0],
values[1]))
```

We'll now write the following content onto a file:

```
Pineapple
Guava
Apple
fruits = ["Pineapple", "Guava", "Apple"]

file_handle = open("fruits.txt", "w")
```

for fruit in fruits:

```
        file_handle.write("{}\n".format(fruit))

file_handle.close()
```

Line 1 – the content we want to be written in a list is kept in a list named 'fruits.'

Line 3 – the file called 'fruits.txt' is opened for writing (w)

Line 5 – each fruit in the list is looped through

Line 6 – each fruit is written. Note the addition of a newline character, \n, for each write; this ensures a new line is used for each fruit

Line 8 – once we are done, we exit the loop, and the file is closed.

That brings us to the end of this quick primer. As you saw, if you already have a background in Python, you won't need to go over this chapter and can go straight to chapter two. This really just gives you an overview of what you will need to know when you start machine learning.

Chapter 2

Machine Learning Fundamentals

The idea of artificial intelligence came from the thought that machines can think intelligently like humans, mimicking the process of human thought and the way we learn. It comes from the thought that machines can adapt quite easily to new inputs, performing tasks without needing human intervention.

Central to artificial intelligence is machine learning, and it focuses mostly on the machine's capability, engineered by humans, to learn and to self-train. They do this by finding patterns in data, improve the algorithm underlying the processing, making independent decisions, again without the need for humans to interfere.

The term 'machine learning' was first coined in 1959 by Arthur Samuel, a pioneering AI and gaming expert, when he worked at IBM.

The hypothesis behind machine learning is that we can use targeted data to train modern computers, and we can adapt that data to whatever functionality we require. Machine learning is wholly driven by pattern recognition – the machine will record them and go back to past data and results to compare and learn from. Given that we expect machines to process vast amounts of data, they need to be adaptable to new data without any need for a human to program them and that is where the iterative side of machine learning comes into play.

Right now, machine learning is one of the hottest topics, not just in the scientific world, but in business and academia. That has led to several definitions, and these are some of the more common ones from reputable sources:

- *"Machine learning is the science of getting computers to act without being explicitly programmed."* – Stanford University

- *"The field of Machine Learning seeks to answer the question, how can we build computer systems that automatically improve with experience, and what are the fundamental laws that govern all learning processes?"* – Carnegie Mellon University

- *"Machine learning algorithms can figure out how to perform important tasks by generalizing from examples."* – University of Washington

- *"Machine Learning, at its most basic, is the practice of using algorithms to parse data, learn from it, and then make a determination or prediction about something in the world."* – Nvidia

- *"Machine learning is based on algorithms that can learn from data without relying on rules-based programming."* – McKinsey.

Fundamental Concepts

One of machine learning's biggest draws is the capability to learn automatically from data, rather than having to manually construct programs specifically for the machine. The last ten years has seen a significant rise in the use of machine learning algorithms and, while they may have started out as a part of the scientific community only, now they are in use everywhere, in every industry, across the entire globe.

These algorithms can generalize tasks so they can be iteratively executed. It takes serious time and money to construct programs for every specific task, and it isn't always possible to do. With machine learning, programming is far more cost-effective, convenient and much easier to do. Machine learning is already being used to tackle important issues, such as the depletion of water levels underground and global warming and, so far, it is looking like a promising system, with the collection of vast amounts of relevant data.

There is more than one type of machine learning in existence, but the fundamental concepts are largely the same – representation, evaluation, and optimization. Here are those three concepts explained:

Representation

Machine learning models lack three primary features – they cannot directly hear, see, or sense any input example. Because of that, the model must be supplied with a data representation to give it the insight it needs into the data, and draw out the important qualities. It is vital that a decent range of key features, offering the best data representation, are used to train the machine learning model.

Representation means nothing more sinister than representing the key points to the computer, using a language the computer can understand, and that's done using classifiers.

We can define classifiers as systems that "input vectors containing discrete and/or continuous values, and outputting one discrete value called a class." For models to learn from that data, the hypothesis space (the set of training data) must have the required classifier the model is being trained on. If a classifier is outside the hypothesis space, the model cannot learn it.

One of the most critical points in the entire machine learning process is the data features used for representing the input. They are so important that they can and typically are the difference between success and failure of a project.

If the data set used for training the model has plenty of independent features, all with a good relationship with the 'class,' the training is decidedly smoother. If the data set is full of complex features, the model may struggle to learn from it. Often, the raw data must be processed for the right features to be drawn from it and constructed into the right training set for the model.

That is one of the most time-consuming parts of the entire process, but it is also one of the most interesting as it doesn't just come down to technical requirements; it also requires a certain amount of trial and error and plenty of intuition.

It should also be borne in mind that this process of constructing the training set and training the model on it is not a one-off. That's where the iterative part comes in; the output must be analyzed, modified where needed, and the entire process repeated, as many times as necessary.

Domain specificity plays a part in the time it takes to build training data sets too. A data set constructed for developing autonomous vehicles will be somewhat different from the one required by, say, an e-commerce company that wants predictions generated, based on an analysis of consumer behavior. That said, the process itself will be much the same regardless of industry.

Evaluation

Evaluation is a process whereby several models are judged, intending to choose one particular model over all others. An important factor in this choice is the ability to tell the difference between vague and useful classifiers and, for that, an 'evaluation function' is used. That function is also called a scoring, utility, or objective function. This is different from the internal function in the algorithm.

Typically, defining the function is done before the data representation tool is chosen and is the first part of the entire project. As an example, for the model used for an autonomous vehicle, the function would include a feature for identifying pedestrians near to it at a low false-positive and near-zero negative; this also sets the condition represented using the right data features.

Optimization

Optimization is when the models' space is searched, looking for a higher soring classifier or a more efficient evaluation. If an algorithm has two or more optimal classifiers, this selection process is paramount to determining the classifier and to ensure the model is the most efficient. There are plenty of off-shelf optimizers that may be used on new machine learning models before a customized optimizer is introduced.

Basic Terminology

You will come across loads of terms during you foray into machine learning so, to give you a helping hand, I've drawn up a list of the fundamental terms you need to learn and understand:

Agent

This goes with reinforcement learning. An agent is defined as "the entity that uses a policy to maximize expected return gained from transitioning between states of the environment."

Boosting

Boosting is, simply, a technique whereby simple, inaccurate classifiers are combined into one that is highly accurate. Inaccurate classifiers are typically known as weak, whereas accurate classifiers are called string classifiers. This is done through a process of 'up-weighting' the data samples misclassified by the model.

Candidate Generation

When a recommendation system chooses the initial recommendation set, it is called Candidate Generation. An example would be a library, offering 600,000 titles. The technique brings up a small subset of several hundred titles to meet the requirements of a user; that subset can then be refined even further if required

Categorical Data

This is when the data features contain a "discrete set" with possible values. An example would be a feature called 'vehicle style' with several, unconnected possible values of truck, car, motorbike, etc.

Checkpoint

A checkpoint is data that can capture the model variable's state at any given moment. Using checkpoints, the training can cover several sessions, with scores or model weights being exportable.

Classification Model

This is a type of machine learning model that takes two or more discrete data classes and characterizes them. An example would be a model built to identify different breeds of dog, using images to determine if the input is a German Shepherd, Poodle, Retriever, and so on.

Collaborative Filtering

This is when predictions are generated for a specific user, based on interests shared between groups of like-minded users.

Continuous Feature

This is defined as a "floating-point feature that has an infinite range of possible values."

Discrete Feature

Opposite to the continuous feature, this is rigid, and the set of possible values is finite.

Discriminator

A discriminator is a system that decides if the input samples are fake or real.

Down-sampling

This is when the information in a feature is reduced or when an unreasonably low percentage of over-represented samples are used for more efficient training of the ML model.

Dynamic Model

This is a model that receives continuous input data, resulting in continuous training.

Ensemble

The prediction set that results from the predictions from several models being merged.

Environment

Again, for reinforcement learning, the environment is where the agent is contained and where it observes the state of its area.

Episode

For reinforcement learning, an episode is all of the iterative tries the agent makes to learn from the environment.

Feature

A feature is a data variable (input) used for prediction generation.

Feature Engineering

The process by which the useful features for training a model are determined and the raw data from the log files converted into those features.

Feature Extraction

This is the process of getting the 'intermediate' representations that a pre-trained or unsupervised machine learning model has calculated and using them as the input in a different model.

Few-Shot Learning

An approach that is typically used for classifying objects and designed, so it learns the best classifiers from a minimal set of training data.

Fine-Tuning

A process of adjusting the parameters of a model that has already been trained, so they fit a different model. This is typically used for refitting weights from an unsupervised to a supervised model.

Generalization

This is the ability that the model has to take new, unseen data, and make the right predictions, rather than using the data the model was originally trained on.

Inference

As far as machine learning goes, inference is when a trained model is applied to unlabeled samples to make predictions.

Label

In terms of supervised machine learning, the result of a sample is a label. A data set with labeled data can have one or more features, and every sample may have corresponding features. An example would be a data set called house, where the features could be the size of the property, number of bathrooms or bedrooms, year built, and so on, while the label would be the price attached to the house.

Linear Model

A linear model is one where predictions are made by assigning each feature with one weight.

Loss

In machine learning terms, a loss is a measure of the distance between the predictions and their labels.

Matplotlib

One of the open-source libraries in Python, it is a plotting library (2D) used for visualization of different machine learning aspects.

Model

In machine learning terms, a model is the representation of what has been learned by a particular machine learning system.

NumPy

Another open-source Python library, NumPy is a math library containing array operations.

One-Shot Learning

In machine learning terms, this is a process whereby classifiers are learned from one training sample. This is typically used in classifying objects.

Overfitting

This is when a model is created with such a close match to the training data that it cannot make any predictions on new and/or unseen data.

Parameter

A parameter is a model variable used by an ML system to train by itself.

Pipeline

In machine learning terms, a pipeline is an infrastructure around an algorithm, including data collection, adding the data to the training set, training models, and exporting them to production.

Random Forest

A random forest is an 'ensemble approach' that finds the right decision tree with the best fit to the training data. This is done by the development of several decision trees with randomly selected features.

Scaling

In machine learning terms, scaling is one of the more common features used to make the value range in one feature match the value ranges of other dataset features.

Sequence Model

This refers to nothing more than a model that generates predictions based on the 'sequential dependency' of the inputs.

Underfitting

In machine learning terms, underfitting is when a model cannot get the training data complexity because it doesn't have good predictive ability.

Validation

Validation is a process that uses a validation set to evaluate how good a model is , as a part of the training process. The goal is to ensure that the model performance is applicable beyond the initial training set.

Different Machine Learning Models

Several machine learning models exist, and we're going to discuss the most popular now.

ANNs – Artificial Neural Networks

The ANN is one of the most commonly used machine learning tools. They get their inspiration from the human brain and were built as a way of replicating how a human learns. A neural network has one or more hidden layers, an input layer, and an output layer. The hidden layer contains units used for transforming input data so the output layer can use it. ANNs are ideal for detecting complex patterns that human programmers simply cannot extract, as well as teaching the machine to recognize those patterns.

Neural networks are also known as perceptrons, and they first appeared in the 1940s. However, it is only recently that they have really been significantly included in artificial intelligence, and that is down to backpropagation. This is a technique that lets networks make adjustments to their hidden neuron layers when the outcome is different from what was expected or hoped for – such as the example of a network to identify breeds of dogs that mistakenly identifies a cat.

And things have changed even more since the deep learning neural networks (DNNs) arrived on the scene. A DNN contains multiple layers, and thee can extract features until it finds what it wants.

Let's see if we can simplify that. Think of a DNN as a factory line. Once the materials have been input (the dataset), they get passed down the belt. At each stop (layer), a different set of features is extracted, only high-level features, though. If the network is being developed for recognizing images, the first of those layers could be set to analyze pixel brightness.

The second layer might use similar pixel lines to identify edges while a third layer could look for shapes or texture. As we reach the next couple of layers, the DNN will already have several feature detectors, and it can work out specific elements in images, and identify those that are usually found together, such as eyes, mouth, and nose.

After this, the network trainers provide the output with labels, and backpropagation is used to fix mistakes that were previously made. The network will soon be able to do its own classification, without human intervention.

Going further, we can break learning down even more into supervised learning, unsupervised learning, and reinforcement learning.

What About Different Neural Network Types?

The answer to that is several, and each type has its own use cases and complexity levels. The feedforward neural network (FNN) is the basic type, where information only goes one way, from the input to the output.

The recurrent neural network (RNN) is another common network, but, in this one, data goes in more than one direction. These have far better abilities for learning data and tend to be used for the more complicated tasks, such as language recognition or learning handwritten samples.

We also have the CNN (Convolutional Neural Network), the Hopfield networks, the Boltzmann machine networks, and many others. Choosing the right one is entirely dependent on what you want to achieve and the data you are using for training purposes.

Sometimes, you may even want to use more than one approach to see what the different results would be.

Overall, ANNs, all the different types, are used for solving problems that need:

- **Classification of patterns** – this is done via assignation of the input pattern to a predetermined class. An example is land classification, using satellite images for training.

- **Clustering** – this is a type of pattern classification but is unsupervised. An example is using defined patterns of input to predict water stream ecological statuses.

- **Regression/function approximation** – this can create functions from given training pattern sets. An example would be predicting the concentration of ozone on the atmosphere.

- **Prediction** – this uses previous samples, set out in time series, or estimating the output.

- **Optimization** – use for minimizing or maximizing cost functions based on predefined constraints.

- **Content Retrieval** – memory recall, even using distorted or incomplete input.

- **Process control** – this looks for ways to maintain velocity under a data load that constantly changes, and this is done by changing the angle of the throttle.

Genetic Algorithms

Genetic Algorithms should be self-explanatory, but, if not, they basically mimic nature's selection theory. They take the traits from the "fitter" solutions and transfer them to the 'less fit' solutions. This algorithm continues to evolve until the best solution to any given problem is achieved. Much like the human chromosomes, each solution gets encoded into a binary string containing the traits of that solution; every subsequent population is known as a 'generation.' The original set is randomly produced and a selection and reproduction process is used to produce subsequent generations.

A subset of the populace gets bred selectively, producing new chromosomes and that selection process is based on the fitness of each solution, and that will include how close they are to the perfect solution, along with 'deterministic examination.'

Genetic crossover is used to achieve conventional propagation, and the result is a trade of chromosomes from two separate parents to produce the offspring. Mutations are inserted into the chromosome, to provide random modification to part of the parent. Propagation doesn't take place as much as it does in humans but it does provide for new genetic material.

Mutation isn't as important as the crossover in the search advancement, but it is important to maintain the diversity of genetics and that is a fundamental factor in the continuation of evolution. Where 'steady-state' algorithms are concerned, the new generation doesn't supersede so many fit members and this ensures the model is even fitter on average. The reproduction and selection cycle is repeated until the criteria for completion are met. For example, that would be when every organism is identical or the optimum fitness level has been obtained, and there are no new results coming from the evolution.

With focus solely on examining fitness and ignoring any other derivative, the genetic algorithm is considered as computationally robust and highly capable of a balance of efficacy and load.

This type of algorithm can also sample vast amounts of code sequences indirectly, even after they have already been tested. Unlike stochastic techniques, unable to search multimodal and noisy relations, this algorithm can store entire solution populations rather than changing one.

Decision Trees

Decision trees are defined as being graphical decision-making representations that look like a tree. They take every factor or condition under consideration, provided it has the potential to influence both the decision and the consequences of it.

The decision tree is seen as the simplest of the supervised algorithms, consisting of three primary elements:

- Branch nodes – each one represents a data set condition

- Edges – each one represents the decision process (ongoing)

- Leaf nodes – each one is representative of the decision end.

Decision trees are the best choice for predictive analysis and have many uses in prediction generation for both continual and categorical variables.

Putting Machine Learning into Practice

Machine learning is far more complex than developing machine learning algorithms and applying them. Take a look at the steps below, which give you a good idea of the steps involved:

Step One

The project goals are defined, giving careful consideration to all the available domain expertise and previous knowledge. It is important not to allow ambiguity to creep into those project goals; it's difficult because, as you go along, you will always find other goals you want to achieve, many of which are not practical to implement.

Step Two

This is the most time-consuming step as it involves cleaning the data and pre-processing it. The result of this must be a data set containing high-quality data samples; the more data you have, the noisier the training data set becomes, and this has got to be eliminated before it can be passed onto the learning system.

Step Three

Next, you must choose the right machine learning model to meet your project requirements. Given the sheer variety and number of available models, this is one of the easier steps to achieve.

Step Four

The machine learning model will be applied to a specific domain and, depending on what that is, human understanding of the model in question may be required for the results to be understood, so long as the learning model is delivering the right results.

Step Five

The last step is the consolidation of the information or knowledge gained from the model, followed by deployment on an industrial level.

This entire process is repeated iteratively, i.e., over and over again, until a practical result is achieved.

Why is Machine Learning so Important?

It's one thing to know what machine learning is all about, but it's another thing entirely to understand its significance in our daily lives. To get an idea of that, it would be easier to understand what machine learning hasn't had an effect on. Every single part of our lives has been impacted in some way by "smart machines;" machines that were intended to help improve human efficiencies and expand our capacities. Both machine learning and artificial intelligence are the primary focal concepts of what is being termed the "fourth industrial revolution," and that could make us question every thought we ever had about being human.

Some of the top reasons that will help you understand how and why machine learning is so significant in our lives are:

- Repetitive learning is automated, and we get more revelations from our data. This is nothing like the robotic automation, driven by hardware robots, that automate manual work; by contrast, machine learning provides for high-volume performance, and consistent performance of repetitive, computer-based work.

- Artificial intelligence is being helped by machine learning algorithms to adapt to our ever-evolving world. Systems or machines are being allowed to learn, to improve on errors they made previously. ML acts as a predictor or a classifier if you like, acquiring new skills in identifying data patterns and data structures. For example, most of us have heard of the machine learning algorithm that backs up a system that taught itself to play chess and to analyze customer behavior data to generate recommendations for certain products. The sheer beauty of this lies in the way the model can adapt and learn from every set of brand new data.

- Machine learning has made it far more feasible to analyze ever larger and deeper datasets by using neural networks containing one or more hidden layers. Think about it this way – a few years ago, it would have been fantastical to even think of something like a fraud detection system that had several hidden layers. Now with big data firmly here, we have a brand new world to play with. You can think of putting data into a machine learning system as being akin to filling your car with gas – the more you add, the further you can go, and the better the results are. Deep learning models work much better with larger volumes of data because they can easily learn from that data.

- DNNs in machine learning algorithms have brought about the highest levels of accuracy seen to date. An example is the rising use of Google Search, Siri, Alexa, and other smart tech resulting in a rise in deep learning accuracy. DNNs are also responsible for a high level of empowerment across the medical industry – cancer is now more easily detected in MRI scans, using object detection and image classification, showing the same kind of accuracy as a fully trained, experienced, radiologist shows.

- Lastly, AI allows for improved use of machine learning algorithms with bid-data analytics. Over time, data has evolved and is now its own currency; when an algorithm can self-learn, it is only a small step away from being an intellectual property. Raw data is akin to being a gold or diamond mine; the deeper you dig down, the more value you can extract.

When you apply algorithms to data, you can get to the right solution much quicker, gaining the upper hand, so long as you remember that, to be a winner, you must use the best data. Do it right and, no matter how many different comparative techniques are in use, the best information will come to you.

In chapter 3, we'll look at some of the best machine learning algorithms.

Chapter 3

Machine Learning Algorithms

Machine learning algorithms are here to stay. A recent study claims that, within the next decade, around 25% of global jobs will be replaced by these algorithms and it's clear to see, from the sheer amount of big data, not to mention better availability of the required tools, such as R and Python programming languages, that machine learning is fast becoming mainstream in the data science world.

One of the main benefits of machine learning algorithms is automation, followed by the ability to self-modify with continual improvement. This is done over time, as more data is learned, and with little to no human intervention. One of the best examples of this is the recommendation engine used by Netflix; the more you watch, the better the algorithm becomes at making viewing recommendations for you. Amazon uses a similar engine.

Data problems in the real world vary in complexity and, to address these, several specialized algorithms were developed, and continue to be developed to solve the problems. Here, we're going to discuss the classification of machine learning algorithms and some of the most useful algorithms in use today.

Algorithm Classification

There are three classifications of machine learning algorithm:

Supervised:

Supervised algorithms are those that produce predictions based on a supplied sample dataset. These algorithms search the value labels associated with the data points, looking for patterns.

Unsupervised:

In unsupervised algorithms, the data points do not have any labels. The algorithm places the data into clusters, describing the structure, and simplifying complex data, organizing it for better analysis.

Reinforcement

Reinforcement algorithms use individual data points to pick an action and then learn, later on, whether it was a good decision or not. The algorithm strategy changes over time, enabling it to learn better and get the best possible reward.

Common Machine Learning Algorithms

There are hundreds of machine learning algorithms, some more common than others. These are the algorithms you are most likely to use:

Naïve Bayes Classifier

You would struggle to manually classify documents, web pages, emails, or any other lengthy form of text-format notes, and that is where Naïve Bayes steps in to help. Classifiers are functions that use a set of available categories to allocate the element value for the population. An excellent example of this is Spam Filtering. This is one of the most common uses of the Naïve Bayes classifier, assigning labels of Spam or Not spam to a series of emails – it's already in use in the email account you use every day.

It is one of the more popular learning methods based on the Bayes Theorem of Probability, designed for the development of machine learning models specifically for classifying documents and predicting disease. In simple terms, the Bayes Probability Theorem is used for the subjective analysis and classification of words.

When Should You Use It?

- When your training dataset is large or moderate

- If the instances have multiple attributes

Any attribute describing an instance must be conditionally independent, provided a classification parameter is given.

Applications

- **Sentiment Analysis** – Facebook is a good example, where the algorithm is used for the analysis of status updates to see if the emotions are negative or positive.

- **Categorizing Documents** – Google makes use of document categorization for document indexing and to look for relevancy scores. PageRank is one of the largest of these, a mechanism that looks at a database that was parsed, examining all pages marked and classified as Important. The Naïve Bayes algorithm is also used for news articles, classifying them as Politics, Sport, News, Entertainment, etc.

- **Spam Filtering** – Many email providers use the algorithm to determine if received emails are spam or not.

Advantages

- This machine learning algorithm works very well with categorical input variables.

- It has faster convergence, doesn't need as much training data as other models, such as logistic regression, when the assumption of conditional independence holds.

- The Naïve Bayes classifier makes predicting test dataset classes much easier and is a good algorithm for multiple class prediction too.

- Although the assumption of conditional independence is required, the classifier has shown good performance and results in numerous application domains.

K-Means Clustering

K-means is one of the popular unsupervised algorithms, used mostly for analyzing clusters. It is an iterative and non-deterministic method of analysis. K-means works on a gives set of data, using a number of clusters defined beforehand, called k. the K-means output is k clusters, and the input data is partitioned among those clusters.

An example is the Wikipedia search results. Say you ran a search for 'mountain lion' in Wikipedia. The algorithm would respond with every page that had the words 'mountain lion, including those that refer to the animal, the Mac OS version, and so on. The algorithm groups together webpages with similar concepts, so, in this case, the algorithm is applied to every page that mentions 'mountain lion,' clustering the animal pages together, the Mac OS pages together and so on.

Advantages:

- Where clusters are globular, the algorithm produces much tighter clusters than any other clustering algorithm, such as hierarchical.

- With a small k value, the algorithm is faster at computing than the hierarchical clustering, especially where there are a lot of variables.

Applications:

- Most of the major search engines, such as Google and Yahoo!, use k-means for clustering similar webpages together, identifying the relevance the search results are rated at. Doing this ensures the search engines cut down on user computational time.

Support Vector Machine (SVM)

SVM learning algorithms are classified into two different categories:

- **Linear** – in the linear SVM, a hyperplane is used to separate the classifiers (data);

- **Non-linear** – hyperplanes cannot be used for separating data in non-linear SVMs. Take facial detection, for example. The training data is made up of a series of images with faces in them and another series with no faces (pictures of just about everything else). Under conditions such as these, the data is too complex, and a representation cannot possibly be found for each feature vector. It is too complex to try to separate all the faces from everything else in a linear manner.

Advantages:

- They are far more accurate in classifying training data

- In terms of classifying future data correctly, the SVM is highly efficient

- The algorithm doesn't make strong data assumptions

- There is no overfitting.

Applications:

The SVM is used by financial institutions to forecast the stock market. For example, it is used for comparing relative stock performance against other stocks in the sector. Relative comparison ensures investment decisions are managed, basing them on the SVM classifications.

Apriori Algorithm

Another unsupervised algorithm, the Apriori algorithm, takes a data set and generates association rules from it. A rule implies that, where item A happens, there is a certain probability that B will also happen. Mostly, the rules are generated in the IF_THEN format. An example would be IF a person decides to buy a new iPhone, THEN they are likely to purchase a case for it. For these conclusions to be derived, the algorithm looks at how many people purchased iPhone cases when they purchased an iPhone. A ratio is then found, i.e., out of 100 people purchasing the iPhone, 75 of them also bought a case.

The basic principle of the Apriori algorithm is this:

If one item in the set happens frequently, all the subsets of the set also happen a lot.

If one item in the set doesn't happen frequently, the supersets also happen infrequently.

Advantages:

- One of the easiest algorithms to implement

- Parallelization is easy

- You can use the properties from large item datasets

Applications:

- **Detection of Adverse Reactions to Drugs** – the Apriori algorithm is commonly used on healthcare data, performing association analysis between which drugs a patient has taken, each person's characteristics, any adverse side-effects they experience, the diagnosis, and so on. The analysis outputs association rules to identify a combination of medication and characteristics that may result in adverse effects with the drugs.

- **Market Basket Analysis** – Amazon, and other major commerce giants online, use the Apriori algorithm to gather insights and predict what items are likely to be purchased at the same time and which products are the most responsive to any form of promotion. For example, retailers may predict that a person who purchases a multicooker is likely to buy a recipe book or other tools that go with it.

- **Auto-Complete** – lots of online services use auto-complete, and one of the best examples is Google. When you type a word in, Google finds other words associated with it, words that are usually typed after the given word.

Linear Regression

The linear regression algorithm is used to find the relationship between variables and the impact that a change in one has on the other – the impact shown is how the dependent variable is impacted when the independent one is changed. Independent variables are known as 'explanatory' variables because they explain the impact factors on the dependent variable. The dependent variable is often known as the predictor, or the 'factor of interest.'

Advantages:
- Easy to explain as it is an easily interpretable algorithm

- Because it doesn't require much tuning, it is easy to use

- One of the fastest machine learning algorithms

Applications:

- **Sales Estimations** – linear regression is widely used in business for forecasting sales based on trend data. If the business sees that sales are increasing steadily every month, they use linear regression to forecast future sales.

- **Risk Assessment** – especially in the financial or insurance sectors, linear regression is used to carry out risk assessments. Health insurance companies, for example, can use it to analyze how many claims a person has made against their age. This shows that, in many cases, the older a person is, the more claims they make on their insurance, and analysis of this kind helps them to make better business decisions as well as accountability for risk factors.

Decision Tree Machine Learning

Let's assume that you have plans to visit a great hotel for a weekend away, but you can't decide which one to go to. Whenever you want to go to a hotel, you ask your best friend, Marianna, if she thinks it's somewhere you will like. In answering that, Marianna first needs to determine what kind of hotels you like. You provide a list of those you have already been to, telling here whether you liked each one or not – that is a labeled dataset for training.

When you ask Marianna if you will like a hotel (H) or not, she will ask you some questions. Is it a 5* H? Does H have an international restaurant? Does the bar at H stay open past 11 pm? Does H have live entertainment? She will ask lots of questions like this so she can get the most information. The answers are YES or NO for each hotel, based on how you answered the questions. In this way, Marianna is a decision tree.

Decision trees are graphical representations that use branching methods to show every possible outcome of any decision, using specific conditions. The internal node on a decision tree represents tests on attributes, while each branch is a test outcome. The leaf node represents specific labels on classes, e.g., the ultimate decision once all attributes have been computed. The path that runs from the root to the leaf represents the classification rules.

Different Types of Decision Tree

There are two primary types of decision tree:

- **Classification** – the default decision tree, classification trees are used for using the response variable to separate databases down into classes. These tend to be more used when there is a categorical response variable.

- **Regression** – a regression tree is normally used when there are numerical or continuous response variables.

Generally, they are used in prediction problems with classification comparisons.

We can also classify decision trees into two more types, based on the target or response variable type – the Continuous Variable and the Binary Variable tree. The target variable is the decision-maker in the type of tree to use for each problem.

Why A Decision Tree Algorithm Should be Used

- Decision trees are used when there is uncertainty. They also help with communication improvements as they show the decision situation in a graphical representation.

- They are also used by data scientists to capture how a model or situation would change if a different decision path were taken.

- They help ensure optimal decision-making because you can traverse through the different paths, forwards and backward.

When A Decision Tree Should be Used

- Because they robust where errors are concerned, and training data has errors, the decision tree is ideal for helping solve the problem

- Also suited to problems where attribute value pairs represent the instances.

- If there are missing values in the training data, the decision tree can be used; they look at the other data to handle any missing values.

- They also work well when the response or target function features discrete values as the outputs.

Advantages:
- They are instinctual, and anyone can understand how they work, even those who are not very technical. The graphical representation of the algorithm hypotheses is self-explanatory and easy to read.

- The data type is not considered a constraint in decision tree algorithms as they can easily handle numerical and categorical variables.

- There is no need for linearity assumption in the data, and, as such, the decision tree may be used in cases where there are non-linear relationships between parameters. The algorithm also does not make assumptions on the space distribution or structure of the classifier.

- They are very useful for exploring data. One of the most important factors in predictive analytics is feature selection, and decision trees implicitly perform this. When the tree is fit to a given dataset, the decision tree is split using the nodes at the top of the tree – these nodes are important variables within the dataset and the default is automatic feature selection.

- Using a decision tree can save valuable time in preparing the data. This is down to the lack of sensitivity with outliers and missing values. If values are missing, it will not prevent the data from being split to build the tree. Outliers also have no effect because the split is based on some, not all, samples in the range of the split; it doesn't use absolute exact values.

Drawbacks:
- The more decisions there are in the tree, the less accuracy there will be in the outcome.

- A significant drawback is that outcomes are sometimes based entirely on expectations. When real-time decisions are made, you may not get the same outcome as expected. There is a chance that an unrealistic tree may lead to significant errors and, where expectations are not rational, flawed decision-making capabilities and bad analysis of the tree; we can't always plan for every potential outcome.

- Decision trees are not good fits for continuous variables and may provide unstable results and plateaus in the classification.

- While they are easy compared to some of the other decision-making algorithms, when you have large trees, with multiple branches, they become complex and take a lot of time to analyze.

- Also, when the trees are large and multi-branched, they are not easy to comprehend and may result in a number of difficulties in presentation.

Applications:
- Financial firms tend to use the decision tree algorithm for option pricing.

- Decision trees are used for remote sensing and pattern recognition.

- Banks use decision trees to determine if loan applicants are accepted or not, based on the likelihood they will default on their payments.

- A popular company producing baby products, Gerber Products, uses the algorithm to determine whether to carry on using VC in their manufacturing process.

- A tool called Guardian has been developed by Rush University Medical Center to identify trends in diseases and patients who are at risk of certain diseases.

Random Forest Machine Learning

Keeping with our decision tree example, we have Marianna as a decision tree for hotel preferences. However, because Marianna is human, she won't always be that accurate at generalizing your hotel preferences. To get accuracy in the recommendations, you decide to ask some more friends and, if most of them say that you will like a specific hotel, you will visit it.

Rather than just asking Marianna, you want to ask Jonathon, Sally, Brian, and Brandy to decide if they think you will like a specific hotel. The implication here is that you have an ensemble – a group of decision trees – that is also called a forest.

Because you don't want the same answer from everyone, you provide slightly different data to each of them. And, right now, you aren't very sure about your preferences and are in a bit of difficulty. You told Marianna that you like a hotel with an outdoor dining option. Now, while this may be fine in the warmer months, you don't really want to be sat outside eating in the winter. So, all the friends you ask shouldn't use that data point, the outside dining, to recommend a hotel.

To help solve this, we use the Random Forest algorithm. A bagging approach is used to create a group of trees using random data subsets. A machine learning model is trained multiple times on a random dataset sample to ensure as near to accurate predictions as possible.

Using the ensemble method, all the outputs from each tree are combined, producing one prediction. In short, all the outputs are polled to produce the prediction, or the model may just choose a prediction that appears more than once in the trees.

For example, let's say that five of your friends determine that hotel H is a good one for you, but another three friends don't think that the prediction will be hotel H because the majority answer will always win.

Why Use the Random Forest Algorithm?

- Both R and Python contain several free and open-source random forest implementations.

- Even when there are missing values, accuracy is maintained. It is also outlier-resistant.

- It is easy to use because the basic algorithm requires just a few short code lines to implement it.

- They save data scientists precious preparation time because no input prep is needed, and they can handle binary, numerical, and categorical features with no need for modification, transformation or scaling.

- The feature selection is implicit as the random forest estimates the variables it sees as vital to the classification.

Advantages

- Overfitting is not considered a problem like it is with the decision trees, and there is no need for random forests to be pruned.

- Most of the time, the random forest is a fast algorithm, but not every time. As an example, when we ran the algorithm, containing 1oo variables in the dataset, along with 50,000 cases, on an 800 MHz computer, it took 11 minutes to produce 100 trees.

- It is versatile and highly effective in many classification tasks and regression tasks because they are less sensitive to noise.

- Producing a bad random forest is not easy. Choosing the right parameters is simple because the random forest does not have a sensitivity to parameters for running the algorithm. It is relatively easy to build a good model without having to do too much tuning.

- The random forest is efficient when used on large datasets.

- You can grow random forest algorithms in parallel.

- It has one of the highest levels of classification accuracy.

Drawbacks

- Although easy enough to use, random forests are not easy to analyze theoretically.

- If you have too many trees in the forest, the algorithm will be slower to make real-time predictions.

- If the categorical variables in the data have varying numbers of levels, some bias will be shown by the algorithm in favor of attributes that have higher numbers of levels. In situations such as this, the scores for variable importance are not terribly reliable.

- Random forest for regression will not make predictions outside of the response value range present in the training dataset.

Applications:

- Banks use the random forest algorithm to predict the risk factor of a loan applicant.

- The automobile industry uses the algorithm to predict the likelihood of a mechanical part failing or breaking.

- The healthcare industry uses it to predict the likelihood of a patient developing a disease.

- They are also useful in regression tasks, such as predicting performance scores and average social media shares.

- The random forest has recently begun to be used for the prediction of speech recognition patterns, and classification of text and images.

Logistic Regression

Some confusion may arise with the name of this algorithm because logistic regression is not used for regression; instead, it is used for classification problems. The name implies that linear models are fit into feature space.

A logistic function is applied to the combination of a linear features and used for predicting what happens to a categorical dependent variable, using predictor variables to make the decision.

The probabilities used for describing a single trial's outcome are then built into a model containing explanatory variables. Logistic regression uses the predictor variables to predict the probability of a certain level of the dependent variable (categorical) being fallen into.

Let's say that you want to make a prediction – will it snow in Canada tomorrow? The outcome will not be a continuous number – it's yes or no. As such, we can't use linear regression.

Logistic regression is more helpful because the outcome variable is one of multiple categories.

Using the categorical response as a marker, we can split logistic regression into three types:

- **Binary** – this is used the most often. There are two possible values for the categorical response – yes or no – i.e., making predictions on whether a patient has high blood pressure or low; if a student will pass an exam, or fail it, or whether a tumor is malignant or benign.

- **Multinomial** – when there are three possible outcomes and no specific ordering in them. i.e., a prediction of the search engine used by most people.

- **Ordinal** – when there are at least three possible outcomes, and there is a natural order to them. i.e., how a service is rated by a customer, how food quality is rated on a 1-10 scale.

Let's look at an example. Let's assume that a bakery sells two varieties of cake – hard and soft – each with several variations, names, and prices. A cake manufacturer wants to find out the optimum baking temperature to produce both hard and soft cakes, considering three temperatures – 150°C, 190°C, and 210°C. Logistic regression is a better fit than other techniques to determine the answer.

When Logistic Regression Should be Used

- When the response variable probabilities need to be modeled as functions of other explanatory variables. i.e., the probability that product X will be purchased as a function of a variable called gender.

- When probabilities need to be predicted for categorical variables falling into two binary response categories, as a function of a different explanatory variable. i.e., the probability that, if a customer is female, she will purchase perfume.

- They are also suited to the need for classification elements into two categories, based on what the explanatory variable is. i.e., the classification of males into the 'young' group or the 'old' group, depending on the age variable.

Advantages

- Not so complex and inspection is easier

- Classed as robust because there is no need for the independent variables to have normal distribution or equal variance.

- There is no linear relationship between independent and dependent variables, which means non-linear effects are easily handled.

Drawbacks

- With high-dimensional and sparse training data, there is every chance the logistic regression model will overfit the data.

- Continuous outcomes cannot be predicted with the logistic regression algorithm. For example, the algorithm cannot be applied when your model goal is to predict the strength of the wind; the scale to measure wind strength is a continuous one. A data scientist could only go as far as predicting whether the wind would be high or low, but that would compromise the dataset precision.

- More data is needed for this algorithm to produce meaningful and stable results. Predictors require at least 50 data points for the outcome to be stable.

- The outcomes are predicted based on the independent variables; if the data scientist wrongly identified the variable, the model would not have any useful predictive value.

- Logistic regression models are sensitive to missing values and outliers.

Applications

- This algorithm is typically applied in the epidemiology field, identifying disease risk factors, and allowing preventive measures to be planned for.

- Used in politics to predict if a given candidate will lose or win or to predict which candidate an individual will vote for.

- Used in the classification of word sets into adjectives, nouns, verbs, and pronouns.

- Used by forecasters to predict if it will rain or not.

- Used by credit score systems to predict the probability of an account being defaulted on.

Chapter 4

Pre-Processing Your Data
and Creating a Training Dataset

Data pre-processing is all about turning raw data into a format that is easy to read. Real-world data tends to be missing some trends and behaviors and is rarely complete or consistent. Very often, attribute values are missing, and the data is full of outliers or errors. Preprocessing it is the best way to solve these issues and, it is worth keeping in mind that machine learning models cannot easily transmit real or raw data. As such, it must be cleaned and processed first.

Here, we look at an overview of the process.

Data Cleaning

Often, data contains a lot of meaningless information and even some missing data. To manage these issues, we clean the data to handle any missing or noisy data.

Missing Data

When some of the data is missing, there are a few ways to handle it:

- **By ignoring tuples** - this is only a good approach to use when we are using a large dataset, and a tuple has many missing values.

- **By filling in the values** – this can be done in a few ways, either by manually filling them in, using the value with the highest probability of being correct, or by using attribute mean.

Noisy Data

Noisy data is data that has little meaning, and the machine model is unable to interpret it. Generation may be via faulty collection methods or errors in data entry, and it is handled in these ways:

- **Binning** – the binning method smooths out sorted data by dividing the data down into equal-sized parts and then performing various methods. Each part is handled separate from the others, and you can use the mean to replace the data or use the boundary values for task completion.

- **Regression** – data may be smoothed out using a regression function. It may be linear, with a single independent variable, or non-linear with several independent variables.

- **Clustering** – all similar data is grouped in clusters. Outliers may not be detected, or they may be outside of the clusters.

Data Transformation

This step transforms data into the right form for the data mining (processing) stage, and this may be done in these ways:

- **Normalization** – this is done to ensure the data values are scaled to specific ranges, i.e., 0.0 to 1.0 or -1.0 to 1.0.

- **Attribute Selection** – the given attributes are used to construct new attributes

- **Discretization** – the numeric attribute's raw values are replaced by conceptual or interval levels.

- **Generation of Concept Hierarchy** – the attributes are converted to the higher level in the hierarchy, i.e., an attribute called 'town' would be converted to an attribute called 'city.'

Data Reduction

Because data mining handles vast quantities of data, the more data there is, the harder it can be to analyze it. Data reduction is required to deal with this, aiming to make storage more efficient while reducing the costs of storage and analysis.

The steps involved in data reduction are:

1. **Data Cube Aggregation** – aggregation is done on the data so the data cube may be constructed.

2. **Attribute Subset Selection** – only the most relevant attributes are needed, the rest can be left out. Attribute selection requires the attribute's p-value and the significance level – the attributes with higher p-values than the significance level may be left out.

Numerosity Reduction

This allows just the data model to be stored rather than the entire data and is often used in regression models.

- **Dimensionality Reduction** – encoding mechanisms are used to reduce the data size, and these can be lossless or lossy. Once the reconstruction has been completed from the compressed data, if the original data is retrievable, it is a lossless reduction; otherwise, it is lossy. There are two main reduction methods – Principal Component Analysis (PCA) and Wavelet transforms.

Data Pre-Processing Steps

Step One - Importing the Library

The first step is to import the data library needed. There are loads to choose from, depending entirely on what your data requirements are. Some of those libraries are:

- **Pandas** – typically used in data manipulation and data visualization

- **NumPy** – a fundamental package that uses Python for scientific computation

- **Matplotlib** – another standard library in Python, typically used for the creation of 2D graphs and plots

- **Seaborn** – a derivation of Matplotlib and one of the most popular visualization libraries

You could use the main libraries in NumPy, Pandas, and another library called time; from Seaborn and Matplotlib, you could use the data visualization libraries and Scikit-learn libraries if you want algorithms and data preprocessing.

I'm going to show you how these libraries are imported:

The Main Libraries

```
import pandas as pd
import numpy as np
import time
```

The Visualization Libraries

```
from matplotlib import pyplot as plt
import seaborn as sns
from mpl_toolkits.mplot3d import Axes3D
plt.style.use('ggplot')
```

The Scikit-Learn Libraries

```
from sklearn.neighbors import KNeighborsClassifier
from sklearn.model_selection import train_test_split
from sklearn.preprocessing import normalize
from sklearn.metrics import
confusion_matrix,accuracy_score,precision_score,recall_
score,f1_score,matthews_corrcoef,classification_report,ro
c_curve
from sklearn.externals import joblib
from sklearn.preprocessing import StandardScaler
from sklearn.decomposition import PCA
```

Step Two – Exploring the Data

The next code gives you an idea of the imported Pandas dataset:

```
"# Use pandas to read the CSV file data
df = pd.read_csv('.'/input/creditcard.csv')
df.head()"
```

Step Three – Look for Missing Values

One of the most important factors is to understand what missing values are; you can't possibly manage your data effectively if you don't. If the missing values are incorrectly handled, you could up with the wrong inferences from the data, and the results will be quite different. There are several techniques you can use for handling missing values:

- *Ignoring the data row*

This technique is used when you have missing class labels, or a row has several missing attributes, assuming this is for classification purposes. That said, if there are a lot of rows with missing labels, the output won't be good.

For example, if you have a database containing student enrolment data, such as name, address, SAT score, and so on, you would have columns with Low, Medium, and High for classifying college achievement. Assuming that you want a model for predicting college achievements, if some of your data rows don't have the achievement column, you won't get accurate predictions so those rows can be deleted before you execute the algorithm

- *Filling in the Missing Values Using a Global Constant*

This technique involves selecting a new global constant, appropriate to the missing data, like 'minus infinity,' 'unknown,' or 'N/A.' That constant then replaces the missing values. We use this technique when it doesn't make sense to put in the effort to predict the values. Going back to the example database for students, let's assume that there is a lack of information regarding the 'state' some students reside in. Instead of predicting where they may live, it makes more sense it use 'N/A' to complete the missing values.

- *Using Attribute Mean*

The attribute mean technique is used for replacing missing values with a mean/median value, so long as it is discrete, for specified database attributes. For example, in a database containing details of income for US families, if a family has an average income of X, you could use that value for replacing the same missing value in the other records.

- *Using Attribute Mean For All Same-Class Samples*

We use this one for restricting calculations to one specified class. By doing this, we can get the value that applies to the row we are looking in for the mean/median of an attribute; that is calculated by searching all the database rows.

Let's say, for example, that you have a database showing automobile prices, classifying them into 'Low Budget,' 'Family,' and 'Luxury,' among others. It would be more precise to replace missing values in the 'Luxury' prices with the average of all vehicles in that category, rather than the value obtained when you add in one or more of the other categories.

- *Predicting Probable Values Using Data Mining Algorithms*

These include regression, decision trees, K-mean, or other cluster algorithms, etc., and they can be used for determining the data attribute's probable value. For example, you could use clustering algorithms to get clusters of rows; you would then use these to work out the attribute's mean/median, as we talked about earlier.

Alternatively, you could use the decision tree for predicting the probable value, taking every other attribute into account.

Step Four – Categorical Data Values

A categorical attribute is only able to take on a specific number of values (feasible), and these tend to be fixed. For example, if you have a user-related dataset, you would have characteristics like age group, gender, nationality, etc. Or, if your dataset is for products or commodities, you could have attributes like manufacturer, vendor, product type, and so on.

All of these are called categorical attributes, and each is stored as a text value. Each value represents one characteristic in the observations. For example, gender is male or female, while you could define product type as food, electronics, and so on.

Categorial data can be split into three categories:

- **Nominal** – these attributes have labeled categories but have no successional order. I.e., gender may be F (female) or M (male) but has no precedence order.

- **Ordinal** – these attributes have labeled categories and an order of precedence. An example would be an economic status feature – these have three categories, low, medium, and high, and these have a natural order.

- **Continuous** – these attributes have categories that are numerical variables. The variables contain infinite values that range between two values that are defined beforehand.

The Challenges Associated with Categorical Data

A categorical attribute may have several levels, known as 'high cardinality.' These levels are mostly in small numbers of instances. Some machine learning models may be algebraic, including the SVM and the regression models, and these need the input to be numerical. First, the categories have to be changed to numbers so those models can be used, and that must happen before applying the algorithm.

There are machine learning libraries r packages that an transform this data automatically int numbers, but that will depend on the techniques embedded in it by default. However, many libraries do not have any support for inputs of categorical data.

Categorical data for computers will not translate the background or any context that users comprehend and can associate with. For example, take a function named City that has several city names associated with it – New Jersey, New York, New Delhi, for example. Most people know that New Jersey and New York are linked because both states are next to one another in America. However, New Delhi and New York are very different. Conversely, the machine just sees the three city names as being three levels of one function. If sufficient context is not given for the model, it will struggle to differentiate between the different levels.

Categorical Data Encoding

All ML models are built using math equations, so it should be pretty easy to understand that it would be difficult to maintain the categorical data in those equations – this is down to equations being driven primarily by numbers. Getting over this requires encoding of the categorical features to numeric quantities.

We're going to look at a few encoding techniques using an airline carrier as an example. The airline carrier is a column from a fictitious database, just so you can understand it easier. These techniques can be applied to any column in any database.

Replacing Categorical Values

This is a very simple technique where the categorical values are replaced with integers. To do this, the replace() function from the pandas library is used and, depending on what your requirements are, the function can easily assign the numbers to the values.

Encoding Labels

Converting categorical values to numbers is known as label encoding. Numeric labels will always be within a range of 0 to n-categories-1. To encode categories to specific numeric values, followed by encoding the rest of the categories to another value is done using NumPy function called where(). For example, al the US airline carriers could be encoded as 1, and every other carrier as 0. You could also use LabelEncoder from Scikit-learn to achieve the same thing.

Label encoding is quite easy to learn and can give your algorithm good performance. However, it does put your algorithm at something of a disadvantage, and your numerical values may be misinterpreted. For example, it may get confused whether a US Airline Carrier with an encoding of 6 should have 6 times more weight than the US Airline Carrie encoded to 1.

One-Hot Encoding

When label encoding is misinterpreted, we can solve it by one-hot encoding. This involves transforming the individual categorical values to new columns and then allocating a 1 (true) or 0 (false) value to each column.

The easiest way to do one-hot encoding is to use a panda function called get_dummies() – appropriately named because dummy data variables are created. Scikit-learn also supports it via OneHotEncoder or LabelBinarizer techniques found in the library's pre-processing module.

However, while using one-hot encoding may solve the misinterpretation issues, it does lead to another problem. When you solve the weight issue by creating several new columns, you get something known as the 'curse of dimensionality,' and the logic that backs this up is that, in high-dimensional spaces, some equations won't work as they should do.

Binary Encoding

Binary encoding will encode all the categories as ordinal. The integers are then converted to a binary string, followed by a division of the binary code digits into columns. As such, the encoding happens in just a couple of dimensions, as opposed to the one-hot encoding where more dimensions are created.

Binary coding can be implemented in an ML model in a few ways, but the best is to install a library called category_encoders. To do this, open cmd on your computer and use the pip install category_encoders command.

Backward Difference Encoding

This method is part of the contrast coding scheme used for categorical attributes. Typically, a K category characteristic will go into regression as several dummy variables, called k-1. The reason this works is that a comparison is drawn between independent variable mean on a level with the independent variable mean from the previous stage. We use this type of ending on ordinal or nominal variables.

The code to use this is much the same as you use for other methods in the category_encoders library, but the run command is BackwardDifferenceEncoder.

Miscellaneous Features

On occasion, you may find yourself dealing with categorical columns and these will indicate what the value range is in observation points. For example, you may have a column named age that has categories like 0-30, 40-60, and so on. There are a few ways you can handle attributes like this but some popular ways are:

- Division of the categorical ranges into a pair of columns. This is done through the creation of a dummy data frame that contains one feature, age, and then the column is split on the delimiter (-) into two, name start and end. The functions used for this are lambda() and split().

- Replacing each range with a selected measure, such as the range's mean value, and this is done using the split_mean() function.

Step Five – Split the Data Into Test and Training Datasets

Machine learning algorithms need to learn from one set of data to generate the predictions from another set. Generally, a dataset is split into two subsets – one for training and one for testing. A typical split is 70:30 – 70% is used for training, and 30% is used for testing. Sometimes a ratio of 80:20 is used; much will depend on how large the original dataset is and what form it takes.

Don't bother trying to split a dataset manually. It's a waste of time as you will never make the split random enough. In the Scikit-learn library, you will find a very useful tool named Model Selection Library to make the task easy. In that library is a class named train_test_split and this will split your data into two random subsets, in the ratio you supply.

When you use this tool, there are a couple of parameters you should consider:

- **test_size** – this helps us to determine the percentage of the input data to use as the test set. The percentage is input as a fraction; for example, if you wanted to use 30% of that data for training, you would input 0.3. If this parameter is specified, you can skip the next one.

- **train_size** – if you don't set the size of the test data, you must set this one. In much the same way as the last parameter, you use a fraction to set the test size, i.e., 0.7 will give you 70% of the data as a training dataset.

- **Random_state** – this requires an integer to activate the random number generator during the splitting process. Alternatively, you could use a RandomState class instance to generate those numbers. If neither is used, the default will be, and this is the RandomState instance that np.random uses.

Let's say that you had a table of data; you could split it into X for independent features and Y for dependent variables and then use this code to split X down into two sets – xTrain and xTest. The same is done for Y – yTrain and yTest:

```
from sklearn.model_selection import train_test_split
xTrain, xTest, yTrain, yTest = train_test_split(x, y,
test_size = 0.2, random_state = 0)
```

That code is telling us that the size of the test dataset will be 20% (0.2) of the whole dataset, while 80% is left as training data.

Building a Machine Learning Data Pipeline

Typically, programmers define pipelines for the data to follow through the algorithm. Each of the pipeline stages uses the data from the last stage, once that data has been processed as required. Using the word 'pipeline' is a tiny bit misleading, though; the word indicates that the data only flows in one direction (unidirectional), but, in reality, all pipelines in machine learning are iterative and cyclical – each stage must be repeated to get the best algorithm.

The environment a programmer works in to build a machine learning model is generally a selected developmental environment, such as Python. It is here that the programmer can test and train their models, using what is known as a 'sandbox,' all while writing less code than normal. This is a fantastic way of developing iterative models that can be launched quickly, rather than having to go through the development of low-latency production systems.

Eight Stages to Build a Data Pipeline

Creating a data pipeline requires 8 basic stages.

The first stage requires you to identify the problem that the machine learning model will solve, along with documenting all the relevant details.

Ingesting the Data

All machine learning workflows or pipelines start with the same stage – the data must be channeled into the database server. What is important here is that raw data is ingested, completely unmodified, so that we have a solid record of the database. That data can come from any source, either via a request for it or from transmission via another system.

The best databases for storing vast amounts of labeled, defined data and raw, unorganized data are NoSQL document databases. The data evolves quickly, and these databases are not required to stick to predefined schemes. On top of that, they provide data storage that is replicated, scalable and distributed.

- **Offline** – data is sent in through the offline layer, straight to the storage area using an ingestion service. This service can encapsulate both persistence and data sourcing. Internally, repository models are used for communicating with data services. In exchange, they provide interaction with the data storage. Once the data has been saved into the database, the dataset is given a unique batch ID and this allows the data to be queried effectively, allows the data to be monitored and to be tracked, end-to-end. For data to be efficient, in computational terms, when it is ingested, it is split between two folds. Fold one is a definitive pipeline, one for each dataset. This is to ensure that every dataset can be processed, both individually and at the same time. The second fold is that all data, in every pipeline, may be divided to ensure that several server cores, processors, the entire server can all be used efficiently.

By distributing this data preparation across multiple horizontal and vertical pipelines, the time taken to perform the required tasks is much reduced.

Based on a schedule defined upfront, the ingestion service regularly runs, at least once per day, or whenever a trigger is encountered. The producers, or the data source, is uncoupled from the processors by a subject – in this example, that is the data pipeline. When collection of the source data is complete, the 'producer system' sends the 'broker' a notification and the response comes from the notification service embedded; the response is the data ingestion. The notifications service also tells the broker that the original data set was processed successfully and is now in storage in the database.

- **Online** – this ingestion service is the entrance, the way into the online layer's streaming architecture, and is responsible for decoupling the data flow and managing it from the source, right through processing, to the storage components. It does this by providing a consistent, low-latency, high-performance functionality. This layer is also a data bus at the enterprise level. Data is stored in long-term raw storage, a level also used as a mediator to the next streaming service for more real-time processing. For example, techniques used for this would be Apache Flume, a data collection service to a long-term database, and Apache Kafka. Other techniques, similar to this, can also be applied selectively, based on the business's technology stack.

Preparing the Data

Once ingestion has taken place, another pipeline is produced. This is a central pipeline used for evaluating the data condition, which means it looks for variations in the format, patterns, outliers, and information that may be inaccurate, distorted, or not complete, correcting what's wrong as it goes through. This stage also has the feature engineering that we talked about earlier.

A feature pipeline has three main characters – extract, transform, and select:

PHASE	INPUT	OUTPUT
Extract	Raw data	Feature
Transform	Feature	Feature
Select	List<Feature>	List<Feature>

Because this is one of the more complex machine learning components, regardless of the project, it is important that the right design patterns are introduced. In coding context, the implication is that a factory technique is used for producing the features, based on specified function behavior, both abstract and shared, and a pattern that ensures the right features are selected at execution time. This would be a logical approach, and both pipeline re-usability and composition should be considered while the transformers and feature extractors are structured.

There are two ways to select functionalities – the user does it, or it is automated. Take, for example, the 'chi-square' test. We could apply this as a way of classifying the impact on the concept label each functionality would have; the lower-impact features could be discarded before training the model. To do this, we identify some selector APIs. Each feature set must have its own ID to ensure consistency in the model input features and the impact scoring.

A data pipeline must be assembled into a set of transformations that cannot be changed and are easy to combine. From this point on, one of the most critical factors in the model's success is the coverage and testing of the high code.

Segregating the Data
Machine learning models have one primary goal – to develop highly accurate models, based on forecast quality and predictions. The information used for this is derived from input

data, but this time, it is new data that was not available in the training dataset. As such, the labeled set is used as a kind of proxy for unknown, unlabeled data in the future. This is done by dividing the dataset into the two subsets – training and test. There are several ways the dataset can be split and the most common ways are:

- **Sequential** - The custom or default ratio is used to divide the dataset into two sequentially; this ensures that there can be no overlaps with any source data. For instance, the training section could be the first 75%, and the test data, the remaining 25%.

- **Random** - A custom or default ratio would be used to split the dataset into two using a random seed. For instance, a random section of 75% would be used for training and the remainder used for testing.

- One or other of the techniques above combines with the data in each dataset being mixed.

- Splitting the data using an injected approach (customized) – commonly used when you need to have strong control over data segregation.

Technically, we do not consider the segregations stage to be part of the independent pipeline, but there is an API for supporting it. For the required datasets to be returned, the next two stages need to call that API.

In terms of organizing the code, for the caller service to choose the right algorithm, you need a strategy pattern. You also need the ability to inject the random seed or percentage. We also need the API to return labeled or unlabeled data so that the model can be, respectively, trained and tested.

Training the Model

Model pipelines are always considered offline, and scheduling could be anywhere from an hour or two to one a day. This depends entirely on how complex the application is. Plus, event and time may be used for initiating training, and not just by the schedulers.

There are a number of machine learning algorithm libraries for training, including ARIMA, decision trees, regression models, k-means, and so on. All of these can make provisions for new model types to be produced rapidly and for making existing models interchangeable.

For parallelization, there are multiple choices:

- The easiest method is having a specialized pipeline for each individual model, which means every model can be simultaneously operated

- Duplicating the training set is another way; this means the training dataset gets divided, and each subset has a model replica. This tends to be favored for those models requiring every instance field for the computations to be performed, i.e., MF and LDA.

- Third, the whole model could be parallelized, which means it can be separated; each individual partition would then be responsible for maintaining some of the variables. This is best for linear regression, SVM, and other linear models.

- The final choice is a hybrid, a combination of two or more of the strategies mentioned above.

What is important is that tolerance for errors is taken into consideration while the model is being trained. Also, to be considered are training partition failures and data checkpoints, i.e., if there is a transient issue that causes every partition to fail, such as a timeout, then they could all be put through the training again.

Evaluating the Model

This stage will always be offline. We can measure what the predictive power and performance of a model is by comparing the predictions the test set generates with actual values, and we do this using key metrics and key performance indicators. For predictions on future input data, you would use the model that fairs best on the test data. We can design an evaluator library with several evaluators; this will generate the accuracy metrics we want, such as PR or ROC curve, both of which can be stored against the model in the data storage system.

The evaluation service asks the segregation API for the test dataset to start the model training and testing. The evaluators that correspond to it are applied to the model form the candidate repository, and the test findings are returned and saved to that repository. For the final model to be developed, you would need to use both regularization methods and hyper-parameter optimization. The very best model is the one that could be deployed and released in the market.

Deploying the Model

The model that has the best or highest level of performance is marked by both the synchronous (online) and asynchronous (offline) prediction generation as being read for employment. The recommendation is that multiple models should be deployed simultaneously. This ensures a smooth transition from an obsolete model to the current one, implying that there should be a timely response to forecast models with no lapses at the time of deployment.

Scoring the Model

Model scoring is synonymous with model serving and is defined as being a "process that generates new values using a given model and new data." Rather than using the term, prediction, we use score because we need to account for the recognizable values as you can see below:

- **Numerical values** – used for regression models and time series models

- **Probability values** – indicative of the probability of a new input being added to an existing model category

- **Alphabetical value** – indicative of a category name resembling the new data

- **Predicted class/outcome** – may also be used as a score, especially in classification models

After deployment, the models can be used for scores, based on the feature data previous pipelines supplied or from a client service. The predictions generated by the models must be of the same high performance and accuracy in both on and offline mode.

- **Offline** – scoring must be optimal in the offline layer for vast data volumes to be accurate, high performance, and of generating what are known as "fire and forget" predictions. Models can send requests asynchronously for the scoring to be initiated but the batch scoring process must finish and the results accessed before the scoring can begin. The data is prepared by the scoring service; then, the features are produced, and additional features retrieved from the data store. The scoring results are stored in the score data store as soon as scoring is finished. The broker is told when the scoring is finished by way of a service notification and the model detects this; the scoring results are the collected.

- **Online** – in this mode, a request is sent by a client to the soring service. The client can request a specific model version to be invoked; it would do this if it wanted the model router to look at the request and transfer it to a model that corresponds to it. In much the same way as it happens in the offline layer, and per the request, the client prepares data, gets the features, and gets other functions if needed, from the feature store. Once the scoring has finished, the results are sent to the scores store and returned to the client via the network.

The results can be asynchronously supplied, depending on what the use case is, to the client. The result is the scores being reported independently of the initial request, and that's done via one of these methods:

- **Push** – once the scores have been got, a notification is sent to push them to the client

- **Poll** – after production of the scores, a low read-latency database is used for saving them; the databases is polled by the client regularly to fetch the predictions.

Monitoring the Performance

The final step is monitor the model performance, and this must be done for every model. For the clients that serve the models, you may want to consider observing some or all of these data points:

- A model identifier

- The date and time of model deployment

- How many times the model got served

- Average, max and min of the how long model service took

- Feature distribution – those that were used

- The difference between the predicted results and what actually came back

You can compute this metadata throughout the whole scoring process and use it for monitoring the performance of your model.

The performance monitoring service is an offline pipeline which gets a notification of service after a new prediction is made; it will then processed to evaluate the model performance at the same time as persisting the result and raising notifications that are required. A comparison is drawn between the results to assess the training set output and, or performance modeling, several methods could be used, including logging analytics, such as Splunk, Grafana, and Kibana.

A model that has low performance and cannot generate the predictions at a high enough speed will result in the scores being produced by the previous model; that will ensure the solution remains resilient. A strategy is applied, one of being wring rather than let, and the implication is that, if extra time is needed to compute a feature, the previous model will replace it rather than holding up the prediction.

Plus, the score results are connected to the actual, real results as they become accessible. The implication is continuous precision measurement and simultaneous handling of deterioration in speed – this is done by going back to the model before. You can use a chain of responsibility pattern to connect the versions.

It is an ongoing job, monitoring model performance when you consider that one simple modification can bring about reorganization in the structure of a model. Keep in mind that the advantages of any model are defined by how it can generate forecasts and predictions with high speed and accuracy.

Chapter 5

Let's Use Scikit-Learn

It's time to get a little practical and where better to start than Scikit-learn, one of the top machine libraries for Python.

Scikit-learn contains many different algorithms, including random forests, SVM, k-neighbors, and more. On top of that, it has support for NumPy, SciPy, and other scientific and numerical Python libraries

Rather than throwing a whole lot of theory at you, in this chapter, I want to show you how to use Scikit-learn to apply machine learning, and to do that, we need some data. We'll use a data set called Sales_Win_Loss that comes from the IBM Watson data repository. We'll import it using pandas, we'll explore it using pandas methods, and then we'll use Seaborn to plot some techniques so we can visualize the data.

After that, we'll go deeper into Sci-kit learn to see how to process our data and split it into test and training sets. And we'll make use of a handy cheat sheet that will let us determine the best algorithms to use. Last, we will use three algorithms – K-Neighbors, LinearSVC, and Naïve-Bayes – to get some predictions and use different methods to compare the results from the three algorithms. Plus, we'll do a bit more visualization to see the performance scores from the different models.

Don't worry if you are not familiar with pandas – by the end of this chapter, you will have enough understanding to try it on other datasets.

As mentioned, we are going to use IBM Watson's Sales_Win_Loss dataset, containing sales campaign data from a wholesale supplier of automotive parts. Scikit-learn will help us build our model so we can tell which campaign will be a loser and which is a winner.

Let's get started.

Import the Dataset

The first thing we need to do is import pandas into Python. We also need a variables called url, which is where the URL for the downloaded dataset will be stored:

```
#import the modules you need
import pandas as pd
#store the URL in a variable called url
url = "https://community.watsonanalytics.com/wp-
content/uploads/2015/04/WA_Fn-UseC_-Sales-Win-
Loss.csv"
```

The next step is to read that CSV file, and we do that with a handy read_csv() method in pandas. The CSV file contains a list of values, separated by commas and we need it converted to a pandas DataFrame:

```
# Read the data in using `read_csv()`
sales_data = pd.read_csv(url)
```

What you should see from that snippet of code is the variable called sales_data. That is where our DataFrame is now stored. If you are not familiar with panda, the method we used there, pd.csv_read(), will create a DataFrame, a data structure in a tabular form, in which the index in the first column uniquely marks each data row; the first row has a label (name) for every column – these are the names pulled from the original dataset. And the variable called sales_data is structured in much the same way as the image below:

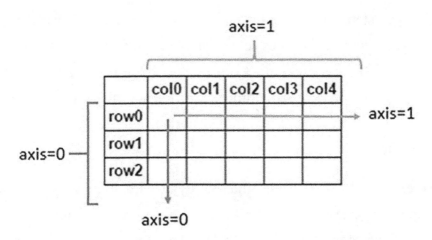

As you can see from this diagram, the indexes for the individual records are row0, row1, row2, etc., and the column names are indicated by col0, col1, col2, etc.

OK, we have our dataset, we've converted it to a DataFrame, and now we want to look at some of the records in it. To do this, we can use a pandas method called head():

```
# use .head() method to see the first couple of
records
sales_data.head()
```

So, the return from this will be the top few records from our dataset. This method, head(), is pretty nifty because it let us to get a feel of what's in the dataset. We'll discuss the method more shortly.

Exploring the Data

The next step is to explore the data we downloaded. We want to see what the data shows us so we can plan where to go next. This is one of the more important steps in machine learning because even the quickest of explorations can tell us things we would miss, and that can lead to some important questions to answer with our model.

To explore the data, we need a few Python libraries. These will help us to process our data so that the powerful Scikit-learn algorithms can use it effectively. We'll start with the method we used before – head() – us to look at the first records of the dataset because it is a powerful method and it can do so much more than just look at data. The head() method is customizable so it shows a specified number of records too:

```
# use the head() method and an argument to help
restrict how many records are shown to start with
sales_data.head(n=2)
```

We've asked the head() method to show just two records from the dataset. The argument, n=2, uses an integer (2) to indicate the second index in the Sales_data DataFrame. With this, we get a look at what kind of data we will be working with. As an example, we could see that columns called Region and Supplies Group have string data in them, while those called Opportunity Number, Opportunity Result, etc., have integers. We can also see that the column called Opportunity Number has got a unique identifier for every record.

OK, now, we have had a quick look at the first records, let's try looking at some of the last records in the data. We can use a different method for this, tail(). It is similar to the head() method in syntax:

```
# use .tail() method to see the last couple records
from our DataFrame
sales_data.tail()
```

You should see the last records from the DataFrame, but we can also customize tail() with arguments so that we see a limited number of records:

```
# use .tail() method and an argument to restrict how
many records are shown
sales_data.tail(n=2)
```

Now, all we can see are the final two records, as n=2 requests. And, similar to head(), the integer of 2 in the n=2 argument is pointing at the second from last index in the two records we requested.

So what do we learn from these last records? Well, we can see, from the column called Opportunity Number, that the dataset has 78,024 records in it. So, what would be good now if we could find out what data types are in the dataset – this is useful information because we might need to do some type conversion later.

We can see those datatypes by using a pandas method called dtypes():

```
# use dtypes() method to show what data types are
available
sales_data.dtypes
```

What you should see is this:

Opportunity Number int64

Supplies Subgroup object

Supplies Group object

Region object

Route To Market object

Elapsed Days In Sales Stage int64

Opportunity Result object

Sales Stage Change Count int64

Total Days Identified Through Closing int64

Total Days Identified Through Qualified int64

Opportunity Amount USD int64

Client Size By Revenue int64

Client Size By Employee Count int64

Revenue From Client Past Two Years int64

Competitor Type object

Ratio Days Identified To Total Days float64

Ratio Days Validated To Total Days float64

Ratio Days Qualified To Total Days float64

Deal Size Category int64

dtype: object

As you can see, when we use dtypes(), all the different columns are listed together with the datatype in it. For example, the

Competitor Type column contains object data types, while the Client Size columns have integers in them. Now we know where the integers are and where the string data is – we can move onto the next step.

Data Visualization

We've done a little basic exploration of the data, so let's have a look at this data, see if we can't uncover any more information in the data. We do that by using plots to visualize the data and there are plenty of libraries that will help you do this – one of the best is a Python library called Seaborn. To use the plots, we first need to import Seaborn, along with Matplotlib:

```
# import seaborn module
import seaborn as sns
# import matplotlib module
import matplotlib.pyplot as plt
# set background color of plot to white
sns.set(style="whitegrid", color_codes=True)
# setting plot size for all plots
sns.set(rc={'figure.figsize':(11.7,8.27)})
# create countplot
sns.countplot('Route To Market',data=sales_data,hue =
'Opportunity Result')
# Remove top and down margin
sns.despine(offset=10, trim=True)
# display the plotplt.show()
```

Seaborn is now set up so we can dive a little deeper into what just happened there.

First, the Seaborn and Matplotlib modules were imported.

In line two, we used a set() method – this helps us to set up the plot properties – color, style, and so on.

We set the plot background as a light color, using sns.set(style="whitegrid", color_codes=True).

Next, the size of our plot was set using sns.set(rc={'figure,figsize':(11.7, 8.27)}), thus defining our plot to be 11.7 px by 8.27 px in size.

Then we used sns.countplot(Route To Market'.data=sales_data.hue = Opportunity Result') to create our plot. The countplot is created using the countplot() method, and this shows us a number of arguments that go with that method. The first argument we used was to define our X-axis. We defined it as the column named "Route to Market and we defined the second argument, which is the data source, as sales_data, the DataFrame we created earlier. The third argument is for the bar plot color – we want it blue for the 'Won' label and green for the 'Loss' label from Opportunity Result.

Now, what does this tell us about our data? Well, for a start, it shows us that there are far more 'loss' records than 'won' records – the bars in the chart show you that. The x-axis, along with the bars for each label, show us that most of the data is concentrated left, towards two categories called "Reseller" and

"Field Sales," You would also see from the plot that "Field Sales" shows more losses than "Reseller."

We chose to use the Route To Market column because it looked, after we studied the head() method and the tail() method, as if it would give us some useful information. But you can use any field you like; any of the others would have given you a plot.

We have a good visualization here of what our data looks like, so let's go deeper and see what we can visualize with some other plots in Seaborn. One of the more popular is called the violin plot and we can use a method called violinplot() from the Seaborn module. First, we'll import the module again and customize it using the set() method – our plot size this time will be 16.7 px by 13.27 px:

```
# import seaborn module
import seaborn as sns
# import matplotlib module
import matplotlib.pyplot as plt
# setting plot size for all plots
sns.set(rc={'figure.figsize':(16.7,13.27)})
```

Now we can plot our violin plot using violinplot() and display using the method called show():

```
# plotting violinplot
sns.violinplot(x="Opportunity Result",y="Client Size
By Revenue", hue="Opportunity Result",
data=sales_data);
plt.show()
```

Now we have a plot, and we can see what information it gives us. A violin plot is used for displaying data distribution across data labels. Our plot has two labels; on the X-axis, we have 'won' and 'loss' and, on the Y-axis, we have 'Client Size By Revenue.' The plot tells us that client size '1' has the biggest data distribution and the remaining labels don't have so much data.

This is good information because it tells us the way in which the data is distributed, which labels and features have got the most data.

Preprocessing the Data

We now know what the data looks like, so we can start the preparation work for building models.

In our first exploration through the data, we noticed that many of the data columns are strings. However, Scikit-learn algorithms don't understand strings, only numeric data. Thankfully, there is an easy way to convert string data into numeric data, using methods supplied in the Scikit-learn library. One of the methods is called LabelEncoder(), and we can use this to turn the categorical labels to numerical labels.

To make this a little easier to understand, look at the next couple of images. The first is a DataFrame with one column called 'Color,' and it has three records Red, Blue, and Green.

	Color
0	Red
1	Green
2	Blue

Our algorithms won't understand this because this is string data; we need numeric data, so the labels, Red, Blue, and Green, need to be converted. Once done, it would look like this:

	Color
0	1
1	2
2	3

Now we know what we're doing, we can start doing it. LabelEncoder() gives us a neat method called fit_transform(); we can use this for encoding our categorical labels into numeric labels. User-defined labels are given to the fit_transform() method as inputs and encoded labels are returned. Let's see an example of how the encoding happens. In the code, we have a list of popular cities, and we want to encode them into something that a machine algorithm can understand.

```
#import necessary module
from sklearn import preprocessing
# create the Labelencoder object
le = preprocessing.LabelEncoder()
#convert categorical columns into numeric
```

```
encoded_value = le.fit_transform(["new york", "new
york", "budapest", "hamburg"])
print(encoded_value)
[2, 2, 0, 1]
```

And there you have it; the string labels have been converted into numeric labels, but how did we do it?

First, the preprocessing module was imported; this is how we got the LabelEncoder() method.

Next, an object was created, one that represented the type of the LabelEncoder() method.

Then, we used the fit_transform() method from that object to tell the difference between the unique classes in the list and returned a list that encoded each entry with a unique value.

You may have noticed that LabelEncoder() assigns the classes with numeric values using the first letter of each class from the list – '(b)udapest' gets a 0 as it is first alphabetically, '(h)amburg' gets a 1, and '(n)ew york' gets a 2.

We have a pretty good understanding of the way LabelEncoder() works now so we can move on. We'll use the method to encode our categorical labels from the DataFrame called sales_data and convert them into numeric values.

We noticed that our columns named Route To Market, Supplies Subgroup, Opportunity Result, Region, Supplies Group, and Competitor Type all had string values. Before we begin to encode them, let's look quickly at the labels contained in each column:

```
print("Supplies Subgroup' : ",sales_data['Supplies
Subgroup'].unique())
print("Region : ",sales_data['Region'].unique())
print("Route To Market : ",sales_data['Route To
Market'].unique())
print("Opportunity Result : ",sales_data['Opportunity
Result'].unique())
print("Competitor Type : ",sales_data['Competitor
Type'].unique())
print("'Supplies Group : ",sales_data['Supplies
Group'].unique())
```

Supplies Subgroup' : ['Exterior Accessories' 'Motorcycle Parts' 'Shelters & RV'

'Garage & Car Care' 'Batteries & Accessories' 'Performance Parts'

'Towing & Hitches' 'Replacement Parts' 'Tires & Wheels'

'Interior Accessories' 'Car Electronics']

Region : ['Northwest' 'Pacific' 'Midwest' 'Southwest' 'Mid-Atlantic' 'Northeast'

'Southeast']

Route To Market : ['Fields Sales' 'Reseller' 'Other' 'Telesales' 'Telecoverage']

Opportunity Result : ['Won' 'Loss']

Competitor Type : ['Unknown' 'Known' 'None']

'Supplies Group : ['Car Accessories' 'Performance & Non-auto' 'Tires & Wheels'

'Car Electronics']

Now all our categorical columns from the DataFrame are laid out, along with the unique classes for each column, we can encode them to numeric labels. We do that with the code example below:

```
#import necessary module
from sklearn import preprocessing
# create Labelencoder object
le = preprocessing.LabelEncoder()
#convert categorical columns to numeric
sales_data['Supplies Subgroup'] =
le.fit_transform(sales_data['Supplies Subgroup'])
sales_data['Region'] =
le.fit_transform(sales_data['Region'])
sales_data['Route To Market'] =
le.fit_transform(sales_data['Route To Market'])
sales_data['Opportunity Result'] =
le.fit_transform(sales_data['Opportunity Result'])
sales_data['Competitor Type'] =
le.fit_transform(sales_data['Competitor Type'])
sales_data['Supplies Group'] =
le.fit_transform(sales_data['Supplies Group'])
#display the initial records
sales_data.head()
```

What happened here?

The preprocessing module was imported, giving us the LabelEncoder() method.

An object was created of a type that represents the LabelEncoder() type.

Then the fit_transform method was used to convert the labels in the columns to numeric labels. BY doing this, all string type columns have now been given a numeric encoding.

Our data is nearly ready to help us build the model, but there is one more very important thing we need to do.

Creating our Training and Test Sets

All machine learning algorithms must be trained on one set of data so that they learn what the relationships are between features, along with the effect the features have on the target variable. Our dataset must be split into two subsets – one for training and one for testing. The training set is, obviously, what the algorithm is trained on, and the test set is what we use to test the model predictions for accuracy.

Before we can split the database, we need to separate out the target variables and the features. First, run the next code:

```
# select columns other than 'Opportunity
Number','Opportunity Result'cols = [col for col in
```

```
sales_data.columns if col not in ['Opportunity
Number','Opportunity Result']]
# dropping 'Opportunity Number' and 'Opportunity
Result' columns
data = sales_data[cols]
#assigning Opportunity Result column as target
target = sales_data['Opportunity Result']
data.head(n=2)
```

OK, what happened here?

First, we no longer require the column called Opportunity Number – it is only a unique identifier for the individual records. Plus, what we want to predict is Opportunity Result, so, rather than having it as a part of the data, we want it as the target. In our first column, we only chose the names that didn't match with Opportunity Result and Opportunity Number and assigned them all to a variable named cols.

Then a new DataFrame data was created, and the columns placed in a list named cols – this will be the feature set. Last, the Opportunity Result column was taken out of sales_data and a new DataFrame target created from it.

That's all we needed to do; now we can define the target and the features into the tow different DataFrames.

The DataFrames data and the target will be split into training and test sets. We will retain 30% of our data for testing, and 70% will go for training data. Obviously, when you start working on your own models, that split will depend on what your data is and what you are trying to achieve.

To split the data, we use a Scikit-learn method called train_test_split():

```
#import necessary module
from sklearn.model_selection import train_test_split
#split data set into train and test sets data_train,
data_test, target_train, target_test =
train_test_split(data,target, test_size = 0.30,
random_state = 10)
```

We now have a test set and a training set.

We imported the module and used the method, train_test_split(), to split our data the way we specified. The training set is data_train, target_train, and the test set is data_test, data_train.

The train_test_split() method's first argument indicates the features we wanted separated out from the previous section, and the second argument indicates the target, in this case, Opportunity Result. The third one specified the percentage for testing data – we used 30% - and the fourth, random_state. is making sure that the results we get every time are reproducible.

Now we are finally ready to build our prediction model.

Building Our Model

Scikit-learn provides a useful tool on their website called a machine_learning_map – it looks like the image below, and we can use it when we want to pick an algorithm:

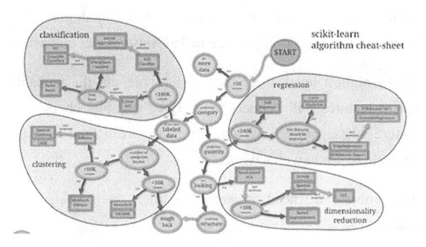

This will help you to pick the algorithms you want to try building the model with. Based on the data we are using, the fact that we have more than 50 samples, we want a category predicted, and our data is labeled, we are going to try three algorithms:

- Naïve Bayes

- Linear SVC

- K-Neighbors Classifier

Scikit-learn offers a whole heap of APIs for the algorithms. This makes it easy for us to try lots of different ones, comparing how accurate they are and working out what is best for our requirements.

We'll go through these algorithms one at a time.

Naïve-Bayes

In Scikit-learn, you will find some classification algorithms that assume, 'naïvely' as it happens, that each feature pair in a dataset is independent. That assumption is what underlies Bayes Theorem, and the algorithms are called Naïve Bayes classifiers.

At the highest level, these algorithms work out the probability that a features will connect to a target variable, choosing the feature whose probability is the highest. We'll look at a quick example to see how this works.

The problem we need answering is this – is it going to rain today?

We've got some data about the weather; we'll use this as the feature set. The target variable is the probability that it will rain. We can use the feature set to come up with table that shows us how often a pair of features and targets happen and it would look like this:

Weather	Rain
Partially Cloudy	No
Cloudy	Yes
Partially Cloudy	No
Partially Cloudy	Yes
Partially Cloudy	Yes
Cloudy	Yes
Total	6

In this table, the feature column is called Weather, and, in it, there are two primary labels – Cloudy and Partially Cloudy. In the Rain column, we can see what the occurrence is of rain happening with a particular weather label. If it does rain when it is cloudy or partially cloudy, we get a Yes; if it doesn't, we get a No.

Now that data can be used for another table, the Frequency Table, where we can see how many times Yes and No were recorded against the related feature:

Frequency		
Weater	No	Yes
Partially Cloudy	2	2
Cloudy	0	2
Total	2	4

Lastly, we take the data from both tables and create another one – the Likelihood table. In this one, we get the number of Yes and No answers and use it to work out what the probability is that each feature will contribute to rain:

Likelihood				
Weather	No	Yes	Individual Probability	
Partially Clody	2	2	4/6	0.6666666667
Cloudy	0	2	2/6	0.3333333333
Total	2	4		
Total Probability	2/6	4/6		
	0.3333333333	0.6666666667		

In the table, we have a column named Individual Probability. In the Occurrence table, Cloudy and Partially Cloudy occurred six times, and, from the Likelihood table, we can see that there were four occurrences of partially Cloudy - two for Yes and two for No. When the occurrences for Yes and No for any given features are divided with the Occurrence table total, the result is a probability for the feature.

What we want to find out is which of the features has the best chance of contributing to rain, and we do that by adding the total No's for every feature to the restrictive total of Yes's from our frequency table; the result of that is then divided with the Occurrence table Total – that provides the probability of each individual feature coinciding or contributing to rain.

We're going to use an algorithm called Gaussian Naïve Bayes or GaussianNB for short because the concept it is based in is much like the weather data example we looked at. The difference is GaussianNB is a lot more complex in mathematical terms.

We'll start by implementing the algorithm:

```
# import necessary module
from sklearn.naive_bayes import GaussianNB
from sklearn.metrics import accuracy_score
#create object of type GaussianNB
gnb = GaussianNB()
#train algorithm on training data and use the test
data to make the prediction
```

```
pred = gnb.fit(data_train,
target_train).predict(data_test)
#print(pred.tolist())
#print accuracy score of model
print("Naive-Bayes accuracy :
",accuracy_score(target_test, pred, normalize =
True))
Naive-Bayes accuracy : 0.759056732741
```

Let's see what we did.

The GaussianNB module was imported, along with the method called accuracy_score.

Next, a gnb object was created – this is an object of GaussianNB type.

The next step was to train our algorithm using data_train, our test data, and target_train, our test target – we used the fit() method to do this. The targets were then predicted in the test data – this was done using the predict() method.

Lastly, the accuracy_score() method was used to print the score. And that is how you build a prediction model applying a Naïve Bayes algorithm to your dataset.

Now let's try the other two algorithms and see how they perform.

LinearSVC

The LinearSVC algorithm, or Linear Support Vector Classification, is an SVM class subclass. At its simplest level, this algorithm attempts to split the data into different planes, looking for the best group it an find of different classes. To understand this better, have a look at the image below – it shows a dataset containing a series of squares and dots. They have been split into a pair of dimensional spaces, located on a pair of axes:

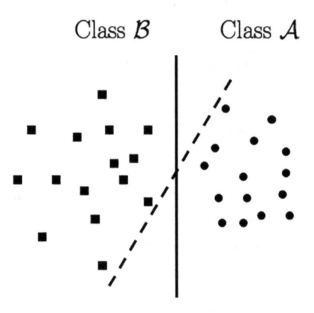

In this image, an implementation of a LinearSVC attempts to slit the 2D space in a way that the dots and the squares (the two data classes) are divided clearly. The lines are presenting divisions that the algorithm attempts to implement as a way of separating the classes available.

Let's get into it:

```
#import necessary modules
```

```
from sklearn.svm import LinearSVC
from sklearn.metrics import accuracy_score
#create object of type LinearSVC
svc_model = LinearSVC(random_state=0)
#train algorithm on training data and use testing
data to make prediction
pred = svc_model.fit(data_train,
target_train).predict(data_test)
#print accuracy score of model
print("LinearSVC accuracy :
",accuracy_score(target_test, pred, normalize =
True))
LinearSVC accuracy : 0.777811004785
```

Much like the GaussianNB model, we started by implementing the modules we needed.

Next, a svc_module type object was created and we set it with a random_state of 0. But, let's just stop there for a minute. What on earth is a random_state? In simple terms, it is nothing more than an instruction, telling the random number generator that the data must be shuffled in a particular order.

In the next step, the LinearSVC algorithm was trained on the training data, and the test data was used to predict our target.

Lastly, the accuracy_score method checked the algorithm's accuracy score.

And now, our last algorithm, the K-nearest neighbors classification algorithm.

K-Neighbors Classifier

This algorithm is more complex than the others so, rather than getting into the complexities of how it works, we'll use the KneighborsClassifier class from Scikit-learn.

Let's get on with implementing it and seeing the way it scores the dataset.

```
#import necessary modules
from sklearn.neighbors import KNeighborsClassifier
from sklearn.metrics import accuracy_score
#create object of classifier
neigh = KNeighborsClassifier(neighbors=3)
#Train algorithm
neigh.fit(data_train, target_train)
# predict response
pred = neigh.predict(data_test)
# evaluate accuracy
print ("KNeighbors accuracy score :
",accuracy_score(target_test, pred))
KNeighbors accuracy score : 0.814550580998
```

This implementation is much the same as the first two.

The modules were implemented and then a neigh object was created of KneighborsClassifier type. We set n_neighbors=3 as the number of neighbors.

Next, the fit() method was used for training the algorithm on our training dataset, testing it on the test data. Lastly, the accuracy score was printed.

All three of our algorithms have been implemented, so the next step is to compare the accuracy scores. We do this to find the model with the best score which means it is the most accurate.

Wouldn't it be better if we had a way of comparing the performance visually? We can do that using a Scikit-learn library called yellowbrick. That library gives us the methods we need for visual presentation of the scoring.

Comparing the Performance

When we implemented our algorithms, we measured our algorithm accuracy using accuracy_score(). This time, the class called ClassificationReport from yellowbrick will give us a visual of the performance and accuracy.

GaussianNB

Starting with GaussianNB

```
from yellowbrick.classifier import
ClassificationReport
# Instantiate classification model and visualizer
visualizer = ClassificationReport(gnb,
classes=['Won','Loss'])
visualizer.fit(data_train, target_train) # Fit
training data to visualizer
visualizer.score(data_test, target_test) # Evaluate
model on test data
g = visualizer.poof() # Draw/show/poof data
```

What we did here was imported ClassificationReport from the module called yellowbrick.classifier.

Next, we create a ClassificationReport type object called visualizer. We pass an argument of a gnb object of ClassificationReport type – remember, we created this in our Naïve Bayes implementation. We passed a second argument which has the Won and Loss labels from the column called Opportunity Result in our DataFrame, sales_data.

The fit() method was used for training our visualizer object then the score() method was used, with the gnb object, to make the predictions as per our algorithm, followed by calculation the prediction accuracy scores.

Lastly, the poof() method drew the plot showing all the scores for the algorithm. The scores are shown against both the Loss and Won labels, allowing us to see the scores over the targets.

LinearSVC

Much like what we've just done, we'll now plot the scores for our LinearSVC algorithm:

```
from yellowbrick.classifier import
ClassificationReport
# Instantiate classification model and visualizer
visualizer = ClassificationReport(svc_model,
classes=['Won','Loss'])
visualizer.fit(data_train, target_train) # Fit
training data to visualizer
```

```
visualizer.score(data_test, target_test) # Evaluate
model on test data
g = visualizer.poof() # Draw/show/poof data
```

We imported the class called ClassificationReport from the module called yellowbrick.classifier. Then we created visualizer, an object of ClassificationReport type. We passed an argument of svc_model, which is a LinearSVC object we created earlier. The next argument has the Won and Loss labels from the sales_data column called Opportunity Result.

The fit()method was used for training our svc_model object and then the score() method makes use of svc_model to make the predictions as per the algorithm. The accuracy scores were calculated and then the poof() method drew the scores plot.

KNeighborsClassifier

Now we'll repeat all of that for our last algorithm:

```
from yellowbrick.classifier import
ClassificationReport
# Instantiate classification model and visualizer
visualizer = ClassificationReport(neigh,
classes=['Won','Loss'])
visualizer.fit(data_train, target_train) # Fit
training data to visualizer
visualizer.score(data_test, target_test) # Evaluate
model on test data
g = visualizer.poof() # Draw/show/poof data
```

Again, we imported ClassificationReport from yellowbrick.classifier. Then we created the visualizer object of the ClassificationReport type and passed an initial argument – a neigh object of KneighborsClassifier type, created when we implemented the algorithm earlier. The next argument has the Won and Loss labels from the sales_data Opportunity Result column.

The fit()method trained our object called neigh and the predictions were made as per the algorithm. Then the accuracy score was calculated and the poof() method drew the scores plot for us.

That's all of our scores visualized; now we can compare them and see which algorithm is the best one.

The Scikit-learn library gives us plenty of algorithms, easily imported into your code, and used for building machine learning models. This works in the same way as any other Python library would be imported and Scikit-learn gives us an incredibly easy way of building and comparing models to find the right one.

We really only touched on what Scikit-learn can do for us here, but there are plenty of online resources that can take your learning further. The best way to learn it is to use it on different datasets – there are lots of open-source ones on the net that you can use – and build your models.

Chapter 6

Using TensorFlow to Build Neural Networks

To finish off the practical side of things, we'll take a walk through TensorFlow and see how we use it to build neural networks. I have based this section on the beginner notebook for TensorFlow 2.0. Do look at it and run it in Google Colab – it isn't big, only 16 code lines – but it will help you understand what we're doing here.

By the end of this chapter, you should understand the important concepts surrounding TensorFlow and Keras, which is a deep-learning library. Those concepts are:

- Shapes in the neural network layers

- Activation functions – SoftMax, ReLU, etc.

- Dropout

- Logits

- Epochs

- Loss

- Optimizers

And the functions we'll be using from TensorFlow and Keras are:

- tf.keras.layers.Sequential()

- tf.keras.layers.Flatten()

- tf.keras.layers.Dense()

- model.compile()

- model.fit()

The Data

This guide will use the MNIST dataset, the 'Hello, World!" of machine learning and neural networks. It is downloaded from Keras and is a dataset that contains a ton of digits from 0 to 9, all hand-drawn, and all labeled to show the digit the image depicts.

The reason we want to use this dataset is that we want a model that can learn the shapes associated with the digits; once trained, the model should be able to identify labels that weren't in the training dataset correctly.

This is not an easy task. Take a look at the image below – it's labeled as '8', but even humans have been known to classify it as '0.'

140

The model we build will take a dataset of training images as its inputs, and it will attempt classification of each image as a digit from 0 to 9. It the prediction is not correct, the model makes a few adjustments, mathematically speaking, to learn to predict better, One training is done, the model will be tested on a new dataset of images, not included in the training set, to see how good it is and what its prediction accuracy is.

Are you ready to see how this is implemented using TensorFlow?

Load the Data

The notebook will first do a little setting up in the initial cell and then loads the MNIST dataset. It does this using the function called load_data() to load the dataset from Keras. The result is a pair of tuples:

```
(x_train, y_train), (x_test, y_test) = mnist.load_data()
```

What might help is if we see what the data looks like as TensorFlow uses it:

```
>>> x_train.shape
(60000, 28, 28)>>> y_train.shape
(60000,)>>> x_test.shape
(10000, 28, 28)>>> y_test.shape
(10000)
```

Those results indicate that the dataset contains 70,000 images in total – 60,000 in the training dataset and 10,000 for testing. Where you see it say 28, twice, these indicate the image size – 28 pixels by 28 pixels, and each image is a 28x28 array containing the pixel values.

The notebook performs one last step in the data preparation stage – it converts all the pixel values into floating-point values between 0.0 and 1.0. Why does it do this? To ensure the math is scaled to produce predictions for the individual images.

```
x_train, x_test = x_train / 255.0, x_test / 255.0
```

Build the Structure

The one bit of the notebook you may find confusing is where the structure of our model is built:

```
model = tf.keras.models.Sequential([
  tf.keras.layers.Flatten(input_shape=(28, 28)),
  tf.keras.layers.Dense(128, activation='relu'),
  tf.keras.layers.Dropout(0.2),
  tf.keras.layers.Dense(10, activation='softmax')
])
```

What does this code do? It tells us the types of layers the neural net will have. Look at the first part - tf.keras.models.Sequential()

– by calling this function, we are creating a sequential layer arrangement – you may understand this better if I tell you it is linear. The rest of the code specifies the layers we are including and the manner they will be arranged in.

In the next line, t.keras.layers.Flatten(input_shape=(28,28)) is used for creating the initial network layer. Because we want all the image information for prediction purposes, the input layer must contain a node corresponding to every pixel Each image has 784 values – 28*28 – and the Flatten() function creates that layer containing 784 modes; each node has one pixel value for a specific image. If we were using color images, each pixel would need three values – RGB –(Red, Green, Blue), and as such, the Flatten() function would give us a layer with 2352 nodes – 28*28*3.

We see another layer type here – the Dense layer, created with tf.keras.layers.Dense(). These layers provide a dully connected layer, otherwise called densely connected. The difference between a fully connected and a sparsely connected layer comes down to the way information moves between the nodes in the adjacent layers.

In dense layers, all the nodes on one layer connect to the nodes in the next one; with sparse connections, this doesn't happen. So, the Dense() function builds layers connected fully to the layer that comes before it. The first argument, in our case, 138, indicates the number of nodes the layer should contain.

The number of those in the hidden layers, which are the layers not included in the input layer or the output layer, is an arbitrary number but you must be aware of one thing – the number of noes in the output layer equals the number of classes the models is built to predict. In our case, the model is trying to make predictions between ten digits, so the last layer must have ten nodes. This is critical – the output from each of the nodes in the last layer is a probability of an image being a specific digit.

We need to delve into dropout and activation functions to get a better understanding of what this is all about.

Activation Functions

Neural net structure and layers are very important, but we must keep one thing in mind – neural nets do an awful lot of mathematics. Every node will take in the values from nodes in the preceding layer. A weighted sum of the nodes is computed and a scalar value is produced – this is known as a logit. In much the same way as the neurons in our brains fire when an input is received, each node or neuron in the net also fires when it gets an input and we need to specify how that will happen. This is where the activation functions come in – the function will take a logit and convert it to a specific activation, based entirely on the activation function in use.

One of the most common of these functions is the ReLU, and we used it in our first Dense() layer. ReLU stands for Rectified Linear Unit, and what it does is ensures negative logits have an activation of 0, which means they will not fire. At the same time, the positive logits do not change and the node will fire at a strength that is proportionally linearly to the input strength.

SoftMax is another common activation function, and we used that in our second Dense() layer. The SoftMax function takes in the logits that were computed by the weighted sum of activation form the preceding layer, turning them into probabilities summing to 1.0. It is one of the most useful of the activation functions for the output layer because the results are incredibly easy to interpret in terms of image predictions.

There are other activation functions and determining which is best is down to, typically, a bit of experimenting, heuristics, or a combination of both.

Dropout
We've one more piece of that code to explain – the tf.keras.layers.Dropout() line. Dropout goes back to where we were talking about layers and connections, and it is to do with some of the drawbacks that come with dense connections. One specific drawback is that densely connected layers can result in neural nets that are expensive in computational terms.

Each node is responsible for sending information to all the nodes in the next layer, and, as this happens, we see a rise in the complexity of the computed weighted sums exponential the number of nodes in the layers. Yet another drawback relates to overfitting – with the amount of information going between the layers, the data can overfit the model and that will result in poor performance.

Dropout comes to the rescue here, ensuring that some nodes in a specified layer will not pass their information on to the following layer. This results in better computation time and reduces the risk of overfitting. In our beginner notebook, there is a call to Dropout(0.2) that falls between our Dense() layers – this ensures that all the nodes in Dense() layer 1 have got a probability of 0.2 that they will be dropped out of the activation computations in the second layer. Effectively, this turns our model's output layer from densely connected to sparsely connected.

Right, we now know all the components in our model, it's time to see how our structure is looking. We use the model.summary() function for that and you should see something like this:

```
Layer (type)                 Output Shape              Param #
=================================================================
flatten (Flatten)            (None, 784)               0

dense (Dense)                (None, 128)               100480

dropout (Dropout)            (None, 128)               0

dense_1 (Dense)              (None, 10)                1290
=================================================================
Total params: 101,770
Trainable params: 101,770
Non-trainable params: 0
_____
```

A quick check of our output shapes and everything is looking pretty good. Time to compile our model, train it and run it.

Compile, Train and Run Our Neural Net

We've sorted out how we want the net to look, so we need to let TensorFlow know how we want it trained.

Compile the Model

We're going to be looking at this piece of code:

```
model.compile(optimizer='adam',
              loss='sparse_categorical_crossentropy',
              metrics=['accuracy'])
```

We call the function named model.compile() on a model that is already built. It is used for specifying the loss function, the optimizer, and the metrics – don't worry, we're going to discuss all of those now as they are crucial features in the way neural nets produce predictions.

Loss Function

On its highest level, the model we are using was built to learn how images should be classified as digits, and this done through predictions. Then it looks at how wrong a prediction was and adjusts itself to get it right the next time around.

Each type of model will require a different loss function – for our problem, where we use probabilities as the model outputs, needs a completely different loss function to a model making predictions in a dollar price, for example.

In our model, the loss function is sparse_categorical_crossentropy, and this is ideal for problems of a multiclass classification type – like ours. If our model were to predict a small probability that an image matches its label, we would have a very high loss.

Optimizer

We can express what it means to train a model in terms of it seeking to minimize a loss. Loss measures how far off being correct a prediction is – the further from the correct answer the prediction is, the higher the loss. So, a way of determining if a model's performance is good or not is to try and minimize that loss.

As we mentioned, a crucial part of the training is in the revision of the math parameters of each network node, and that is based on the effectiveness of each parameter in the image classification. Using a process known as backpropagation, a mathematical tool is used by the neural net for updating model parameters. That tool is called gradient descent, and it helps in improving the model. I won't go into too much detail because it's outside the scope of this book but, to understand what our beginner notebook is doing, the function called model.compile() has an optimizer parameter that specifies how the backpropagation should be more effective and faster. We used the 'adam' optimizer, which is a common one and works well.

Metrics

The last bit of the function is the specification of which metrics should be used for model evaluation. A useful metric, 'accuracy,' isn't perfect and you should be cautious about using it.

Training Our Model

At last, we get to train our model, and TensorFlow 2.0 makes this incredibly easy.

```
model.fit(x_train, y_train, epochs=5)
```

What this code does is passes our training data, along with the correct data labels. In the model.fit() function, the parameter called epoch indicates how many times out model has seen ALL training data. Why would a model need to see all training data several times? Because seeing it just once may be insufficient for the model weights to be updated enough for the computation of the weighted sums – seeing the data several times increases the model's predictive power.

If you run the code, you will see that, in every epoch, the model will see all 60,000 images from the training dataset. And you can see that, after each epoch, the loss goes down an accuracy goes up – this means our model is improving in its classification predictions.

Evaluating Our Model

Last, we can predict our test set classes and evaluate the performance of our model with model.evaluate(x_test, y_test).

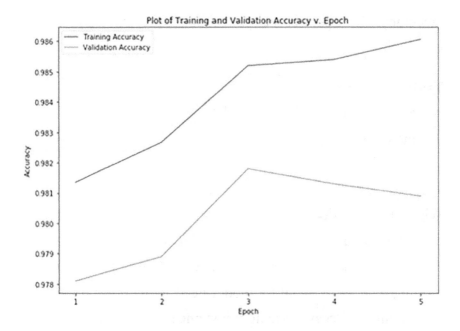

Plot of Training and Validation Accuracy v. Epoch

The plot above indicates that, although accuracy increases with each epoch, the validation accuracy is starting to level out, even decrease; this indicates that five epochs are enough for training purposes.

Well done, on making it to the end of this guide. You should have a much better understanding of machine learning with Python now. Although you don't have all the information you need, you do have enough to give you a basis from which to take your learning to another level.

To finish, I have six tips on helping any business build a successful data training strategy and then you should try the multiple-choice quiz – don't worry if you do not know the answers; I've included them at the end of the book and it will give you an idea of where you need to brush up your skills.

Chapter 7

Six Tips to Help You Build Your Machine Learning Training Data Strategy

Machine learning and artificial intelligence are common terms, heard everywhere these days. Artificial intelligence is all about machines mimicking human thinking while machine learning is the approach you need to learn to create that AI. Let's say that AI is a computer's ability to do a specific task based on specific instruction. That means that ML is the ability the machine has to ingest the data, parse it, and learn from it to make it more accurate at doing the task.

Executives across every industry, from finance to governments, automotive to retail, healthcare to tech, already have a fundamental understanding of both concepts, but not everyone knows how to draw up a proper data training strategy, the most important step in ensuring your machine learning investment pays off.

Artificial intelligence systems will learn by example; the better the examples, the better the system learns. By contrast, give it low-quality data or not enough data, and your system will be unreliable at best and, at worst, produce the wrong results, make very poor decisions, fail to handle real-world variations, and more. It's not only that; using poor data costs; an estimate from IBM indicates that poor quality data costs the USA economy over $3 trillion every year.

If you don't have a decent strategy for collecting your data and structuring it for training purposes, for testing and for tuning your AI and ML systems, you may as well give up – your projects are likely to be delayed, they won't scale as they should, and your competitors are likely to outpace you by a long way.

For those reasons, you need to follow these tips to build the right strategy.

Set a Budget

Whenever you start any new project, you must work out what your project objective is. That tells you the type of data you want and the number of categorized data points you require for your system to be trained.

As an example, if you are building a model to train for pattern recognition or computer vision, your data points would be image data, labeled by humans to identify what it contains. Plus, you may need your model to be trained over and again, continuously, or refreshed, depending on your ultimate aim. You could have to provide updates for your solution – weekly, monthly, quarterly, etc.

As soon as you have identified your data points and your refresh rates, you can work out what your data sourcing options are and draw up a budget.

You must be level-headed here, especially about how long it will take and how much money will be required to get things going, keep them maintained, and evolve, to ensure that your model is always relevant and useful.

Machine learning programs are not short-term investments; you must be prepared to be in it for the long run to ensure you get the best return.

Sourcing the Right Data

The data you want depends entirely on what solution you are building. Some of the options available to you for sourcing data include survey data, real-world use data, public datasets, synthetic data, and so on. As an example, if you were building a speech recognition system, you would need to train it on the highest quality of real-world speech data, translated to text form. Search solutions require text data that humans have annotates to indicate the most relevant results.

There are some common data types in machine learning – video, image, speech, text, and audio. Before any of them can be used to train an ML system, data points need to be labeled, identifying exactly what they are. These labels tell the models what needs to be done with the data. For example, if you had a data item for a VHA (virtual home assistant) that was recording of a person saying, "order more kitchen towels," the label would likely tell the system it needs to order with a specific retailer when the word "order" is heard.

Ensure The Quality of the Data

Depending on what the task is, it can be quite simple to annotate data. However, it is also incredibly time-consuming, repetitive, and not easy to get right on a consistent basis. It needs the human touch.

There are high stakes here; if you use inaccurate data for training your model, the model isn't going to do what you want it to do. Let's say, for example, that you are training a computer vision system. It's for autonomous vehicles, and it has images of pavements mislabeled as streets – think about the results; they could be pretty disastrous!

Data quality refers to labeling consistency and accuracy. Consistency indicates the degree of multiple annotations on data points agreeing with each other while accuracy indicates how near to the truth a label is.

Be Aware of Biases in the Data and Mitigate Them

By concentrating their effort on a high quality of data, organizations can reduce bias in their machine learning and artificial intelligence projects. Bias can easily be hidden until your solution is deployed to the market and, when it gets to that stage, it may not be very easy to fix.

Bias is typically the result of unconscious preferences or blind spots in the data or in the team itself, right from the start of the project. Bias in an artificial intelligence project can come out as uneven facial or voice recognition performance for accents, gender, and ethnicities. As AI becomes used more and more, it is important to address the bias right at the start.

Avoiding bias at project-level requires you to be active in building diversity into your project teams, especially when it comes to the definition of goals, metrics, roadmaps, and algorithms. Yes, it is easier said than done to build diversity into your data team, but you are working to high stakes here. If the team doesn't accurately represent your customer base, the end product is at risk of working for just a small subset. It's not great business sense to miss a huge marketing opportunity and even worse, bias could lead to discrimination in the real world.

Implement Data Security Safeguards Whenever Required

Not all data projects are going to use PII – personally identifiable information – or even sensitive data. However, if you are building a solution that does, you must ensure that data security is built into it. That is even more important when you are working with customer information, government records, financial records, or even content that is generated by the user. Government regulations are increasingly dictating how customer information should be handled and, by putting the proper protections in place, you are protecting yourself, your own data and that of your customers. You must be completely transparent about your practices; they must be ethical, and you must stick to your terms of service. Doing so will give you a huge advantage over your competition; failing to do so not only risks your brand, it also puts you are a risk of scandal.

Choose the Right Technology

The trickier your training data is, the better your outcome will be. Most of the time, organizations will require vast amounts of data, all high quality, fast, and scales. Achieving this requires a solution revolving around a data pipeline. That pipeline will deliver enough volume fast enough to ensure the models are refreshed, and that is why it is so important to choose the right technology for annotating the data.

The tools that you use must be good enough to handle the right data types for your solution; they must allow for flexibility in workflow design labeling, sufficiently manage the quality of individual annotations, manage throughput, and ensure data is labeled by both the model and humans to ensure optimum performance.

Setting the Right Strategy

Almost 90% of organizations already adopt at least one type of transformative technology, such as artificial intelligence. However, only around 26% of those organizations believe that they have the right models in place to capture the full extent of the available value from the technologies they adopt.

The first step towards reaping the full value of these technologies is to have a solid data training strategy in place. Set a sensible budget, identify where your data is coming from, make sure you are using quality data, and that you have sufficient security in place.

Most machine learning models regularly need refreshing, and having a strategy ensures you have a steady data pipeline in place. While a strategy on its own will not guarantee complete success with machine learning and artificial intelligence, it will at least ensure that you are in a better position to utilize the benefits these technologies offer.

Machine Learning Quiz

Question 1 – Applying Machine Learning

When you split a dataset into three, what is the result?

   a) It makes the dataset too large to be trained properly

   b) It makes the dataset too small to be trained properly

   c) It makes the dataset too large to be tested properly

   d) It makes the dataset too small to be tested properly

Question 2 – Machine Learning Test

Which of the following is indicative of unlabeled samples in machine learning?

   a) Prior knowledge exists

   b) There is a lot of confusion in the knowledge

c) The knowledge is not confusing

d) No prior knowledge exists

Question 3 – Neural Networks

What do we use backpropagation for when we train a neural network?

a) To determine how much error is added to the data by each node

b) To determine the weights and parameters the hidden layers represent

c) To determine the error that isn't represented by the remainder of the model

d) To determine which inputs are mapped to the numerical outputs

Question 4 – Machine Learning Test

Why do we use the Bayes Theorem in machine learning?

a) To try to define what the likeability is of an event by using an understanding established previously

b) To try to define what the probability is of an event by using an understanding established previously

c) To try to omit the likeability of an event by using an understanding established previously

d) To try to omit the probability of an event by using an understanding established previously

Question 5 – Supervised Learning

Define what feature bagging is

a) Everything you would want it to be

b) Nothing you would want it to be

c) A random subset of features for every subtree

d) A deterministic subset of features for every subtree

Question 6 – Unsupervised Learning

Which of the following is not one of the benefits of using k-means?

a) K-means may be used for rapid prototyping

b) K-means is simple, and it is fast

c) K-means is useful when you want to preprocess complex clustering algorithms

d) K-means systematically tries the initial centroids

Question 7 – Convolutional and Recurrent Neural Networks

Which of the following describes what a convolutional layer is responsible for?

a) Assigning the weights to a specific area of an image

b) How much needs to be moved

c) New images created when filters are applied

d) Extraction of different features from every bit of an image

Question 8 – Neural Networks

TensorFlow offers two types of installation – what are they?

a) CPU and GPU

b) CPU and Nodes

c) GPU and GUI

d) CUDA and GPU

Question 9 – Machine Learning Test

What does it mean when you use an RBF kernel in SVM with a Gamma value?

a) The distance of the points from the hyperplane for the modeling do not affect the model

b) The model even considers all the points far away from the hyperplane for modeling

c) The model only considers the points near to the hyperplane for modeling

d) None of the above

Question 10 – Machine Learning

Under TensorFlow, which of these Convolutional neural network components perform classification on the extracted features?

a) Dense, or fully-connected, layers

b) Convolutional layers

c) Pooling layers

d) None of the above

Question 11 – Applying Machine Learning

Which of these is not a metric used for the evaluation of binary classification models?

a) Cohen Kapp score

b) Matthews Confusion Coefficient

c) F1 score

d) Confusion matrix

Question 12 – Unsupervised Learning

Which of the following explains the usefulness of the central limit theorem?

a) Normal distribution of small samples of random independent variables

b) Normal distribution of big samples of random independent variables

c) Normal distribution of small samples of random dependent variables

d) Normal distribution of big samples of random dependent variables

Question 13 – Machine Learning

Which of the following is a characteristic of Linear Regression?

a) Models are locally applied

b) Interactions are easily considered

c) It has very small partitions

d) Models are globally applied

Question 14 – Machine Learning

Choose the benefit of using the K-nearest neighbor algorithm in machine learning

a) It doesn't need any training beforehand

b) There is no risk of conflict

c) The predictions are cheaper than other algorithms

d) Including different features ranges has no effect on the distance calculation

Question 15 – Machine Learning

Choose the real-world SVM applications from these:

a) Text and hypertext categorization

b) Image classification

c) Clustering news articles

d) All of the above

Question 16 – Neural Networks

Which of the following are represented in TensorFlow by their elements per dimension?

a) Tensors

b) Tensor shape

c) N-dimensional arrays

d) Variables

Question 17 – Machine Learning

Read the following options:

1. Attempt to run the algorithm to get an alternative centroid initialization

2. Make adjustments to the number of iterations

3. Find out the optimal number of clusters is

Which of those options do we use in the k-means algorithm to get the global minima?

a) 1 and 2

b) 1 and 3

c) 2 and 3

d) All of them

Question 18 – Convolutional and Recurrent Neural Networks

Which of the following isn't a convolutional layer quality?

a) It isn't connected

b) Small image parts are processed

c) It doesn't need any prior training

d) It includes the weight-sharing units

Question 19 – Convolutional and Recurrent Neural Networks

Which of the following doesn't represent logistic units in LSTM structures?

a) Sigmoid

b) X

c) Cell

d) Tanh

Question 20 – Machine Learning

How many components does a Convolutional neural network have under TensorFlow?

a) 2.0

b) 3.0

c) 4.0

d) 5.0

Question 21 – Machine Learning

Choose which of these is a deterministic algorithm example

    a) PCA

    b) K-means

    c) Neither of these

Question 22 – Neural Networks

Which of these is another way of indicating a connected neural network that has two layers?

    a) Feed Forward perceptron

    b) Biased perceptron

    c) Multilayer perceptron

    d) Hidden layer perceptron

Question 23 – Machine learning

Let's assume that we have a dataset and, with a decision tree that has a depth of six, we can train it with 100% accuracy. Now look at the following points:

    1. A depth of four has high bias, low variance

    2. A depth of four has low bias, high variance

Which of these is the correct choice:

a) 1

b) 2

c) 1 and 2

d) None of the above

Question 24 – Supervised Learning

Which of the following is used by C4.5 to determine the level of information available after a split?

a) Uncertainty

b) Randomness

c) Stochastics

d) Entropy

Question 25 – Machine learning

Which of the following does not indicate the quality of a model?

a) Feature engineering

b) Precision and recall

c) Consistency

d) The size of the dataset

Conclusion

Well done on making it to the end of "Machine Learning with Python: Step By Step Methods To Master Machine Learning With Python." I hope that you found it informative and a helpful guide.

Your next step is to take the knowledge you have learned here and build on it. There are plenty of online courses and advanced learning avenues you can walk down and plenty of information just waiting for your eager mind.

Machine learning has been steadily advancing over the years and has resulted in lots of sophisticated technology that can learn by studying patterns in behavior and activity. Now it's down to you to start developing your machine learning model. Use all the resources at your disposal and use this book as your diving board. Take what you learned here and put it to good use.

Thanks once again for choosing my guide, and I wish you luck in your machine learning endeavors.

Machine Learning Quiz – Answers

Question One – Applying Machine Learning

When you split a dataset into three, what is the result?

Answer – b) It makes the dataset too small to be trained properly

Question Two – Machine Learning Test

Which of the following is indicative of unlabeled samples in machine learning?

Answer – d) No prior knowledge exists

Question Three – Neural Networks

What do we use backpropagation for when we train a neural network?

Answer – a) To determine how much error is added to the data by each node

Question Four – Machine Learning Test

Why do we use the Bayes Theorem in machine learning?

Answer – b) To try to define what the probability is of an event by using an understanding established previously

Question Five – Supervised Learning

Define what feature bagging is

Answer – c) A random subset of features for every subtree

Question Six – Unsupervised Learning

Which of the following is not one of the benefits of using k-means?

Answer – d) - K-means systematically tries the initial centroids

Question Seven – Convolutional and Recurrent Neural Networks

Which of the following describes what a convolutional layer is responsible for?

Answer – d) - Extraction of different features from every bit of an image

Question Eight – Neural Networks

TensorFlow offers two types of installation – what are they?

Answer – a) - CPU and GPU

Question Nine – Machine Learning Test

What does it mean when you use an RBF kernel in SVM with a Gamma value?

Answer – c) - The model only considers the points near to the hyperplane for modeling

Question Ten – Machine Learning

Under TensorFlow, which of these Convolutional neural network components perform classification on the extracted features?

Answer – a) - Dense, or fully-connected, layers

Question Eleven – Applying Machine Learning

Which of these is not a metric used for the evaluation of binary classification models?

Answer – b) - Matthews Confusion Coefficient

Question Twelve – Unsupervised Learning

Which of the following explains the usefulness of the central limit theorem?

Answer – b) - Normal distribution of big samples of random independent variables

Question Thirteen – Machine Learning

Which of the following is a characteristic of Linear Regression?

Answer d) - Models are globally applied

Question Fourteen – Machine Learning

Choose the benefit of using the K-nearest neighbor algorithm in machine learning

Answer – a) - It doesn't need any training beforehand

Question Fifteen – Machine Learning

Choose the real-world SVM applications from these:

Answer – d) - All of the above

Question 16 – Neural Networks

Which of the following are represented in TensorFlow by their elements per dimension?

Answer – b) - Tensor shape

Question 17 – Machine Learning

Read the following options:

Answer – d) - All of them

Question Eighteen – Convolutional and Recurrent Neural Networks

Which of the following isn't a convolutional layer quality?

Answer - c) - It doesn't need any prior training

Question Nineteen – Convolutional and Recurrent Neural Networks

Which of the following doesn't represent logistic units in LSTM structures?

Answer – a) – Sigmoid

Question Twenty – Machine Learning

How many components does a Convolutional neural network have under TensorFlow?

Answer – b) - 3.0

Question Twenty-one – Machine Learning

Choose which of these is a deterministic algorithm example

Answer – a) – PCA

Question Twenty-two – Neural Networks

Which of these is another way of indicating a connected neural network that has two layers?

Answer – c) – Multilayer perceptron

Question Twenty-three – Machine learning

Let's assume that we have a dataset and, with a decision tree that has a depth of six, we can train it with 100% accuracy.

Which of these is the correct choice:

Answer – a) – 1

Question twenty-four – Supervised Learning

Which of the following is used by C4.5 to determine the level of information available after a split?

Answer – d) – Entropy

Question Twenty-five – Machine learning

Which of the following does not indicate the quality of a model?

Answer – a) – Feature engineering

References

---

https://www.python.org/

https://docs.python-guide.org/

https://levelup.gitconnected.com/

https://towardsdatascience.com

https://machinelearningmastery.com

https://www.geeksforgeeks.org

https://www.analyticsvidhya.com

https://data-flair.training

https://medium.com

https://www.dataquest.io

https://scikit-learn.org

https://www.tensorflow.org

https://stackabuse.com

https://www.kdnuggets.com

www.ingramcontent.com/pod-product-compliance
Lightning Source LLC
Chambersburg PA
CBHW071154050326
40689CB00011B/2107